GLORIOUS GARDENS

—TO VISIT—

GLORIOUS GARDENS
—TO VISIT—

58 GARDENS IN
NEW YORK
NEW JERSEY
PENNSYLVANIA &
DELAWARE VALLEY
CONNECTICUT
MASSACHUSETTS
RHODE ISLAND

ALL WITHIN
3 HOURS OF
NEW YORK CITY

PRISCILLA DUNHILL and SUE FREEDMAN

Clarkson N. Potter, Inc./Publishers
DISTRIBUTED BY CROWN PUBLISHERS, INC., NEW YORK

Published by Clarkson N. Potter, Inc., 225 Park Avenue South, New York, New York 10003

CLARKSON N. POTTER, POTTER, and colophon are trademarks of Clarkson N. Potter, Inc.

Design by Barbara Peck

Manufactured in the United States of America

Library of Congress Cataloging-in-Publication Data

Dunhill, Priscilla.
    Glorious gardens to visit.

    Includes index.
    1. Gardens—New York Region—Guide-books.
2. New York Region—Description and travel—Guide-books.   I. Freedman, Sue.   II. Title.
SB466.U65N74   1989   712'.025'7471   88–32196
                ISBN 0-517-57212-5

    10 9 8 7 6 5 4 3 2 1
                First Edition

To Vaud, Hank, Mildred, and Emma

CONTENTS

INTRODUCTION
xi
NEW YORK
1

NEW YORK CITY AND ENVIRONS

LONG ISLAND

WESTCHESTER AND OTHER COUNTIES

CONTENTS

NEW JERSEY

89

PENNSYLVANIA AND DELAWARE VALLEY

113

CONNECTICUT

179

WESTERN MASSACHUSETTS

195

RHODE ISLAND

213

INDEX

224

PHOTO CREDITS

224

INTRODUCTION

We are ardent gardeners who began backyard puttering and planting years ago. Our interest gradually metamorphosed from ardor to obsession, first with our own gardens and then with the gardens of others—public, private, and commercial.

In this book we explore the best of those gardens found within three hours of New York City. Our journey is, by design, a personal one, reflecting our pleasures and prejudices. We digress along the way, pursuing subjects that interest us: how garden makers came to make their gardens, an herbal remedy for poison ivy, the mystery of witches'-brooms, or how to espalier an apple tree.

We visited 112 gardens and talked with gardeners, landscape architects, historians, curators, horticulturists, botanists, and weeders. We found people who make gardens to be a passionate lot. They are gamblers and optimists, betting against weather and time that their fragile, evanescent creations will survive. After a hurricane or freak spring snowstorm, gardeners simply pick up shears and shovel and begin again.

The gardens in this book span 250 years. The oldest was begun in the 1730s by John Bartram of Philadelphia, royal botanist to King George III, who explored as far west as the Ohio River to find plant specimens to send home to England. The newest, a community garden along the Hudson River in Manhattan, was planted in the 1980s by 40 New Yorkers.

The gardens range from the terraced showplaces of millionaires to neighborhood plots. All have something special to warrant a visit. All are open to the public, at the least for a few days a year.

We are inconsistent about two things. We vary forms of address—sometimes formal, sometimes casual—according to our perception of the gardener. We have mixed common and Latin names for plants, using common names generally, Latin when the common name is uncommon. *Nostra culpa.*

PRISCILLA DUNHILL
SUE FREEDMAN

NEW
YORK

࿒

BARTOW-PELL MANSION MUSEUM AND GARDENS

BRONX, NEW YORK

࿒ At Bartow-Pell, there's a strong sense of wildness and country. Tidelands spiked with cattails stretch out to Long Island Sound. Birds and crickets sound a constant chorus from the surrounding woodlands. And in the background is the constant low roar of traffic. This is, after all, New York City—Pelham Bay Park in the Bronx.

Throughout the property—even in the 1914 formal walled garden behind the mansion—corners are high with unmown grass, and shrubs sprout with Virginia creeper.

But in spite of this ragged appearance, Bartow-Pell weaves a casual charm. Pink and white roses tumble over the high brick walls. A colorful, if somewhat unkempt, perennial border—astilbe, iris, columbine, yucca, lilies, Queen-Anne's-lace—runs along the base. A sweet herb garden, set neat as a pin in a small half-moon of bricks, interrupts the perennial border and marks the entrance to the formal garden.

The walls of this garden beckon with a sense of mystery. Inside, six colossal yews, each at least 20 feet high and 30 feet wide, brood like some dark prehistoric monsters.

At the center of the garden, a broad frame of flagstones surrounds a large rectangular pool. At each corner of the pool, flower beds bloom in spring with tulips and in summer with red begonias.

Beyond the walled garden, a path leads through the woods to a tiny fenced-in Pell graveyard, dating back to the 1700s.

Thomas Pell bought the land from the Siwanoy Indians in 1654, and Robert Bartow built the neoclassic stone mansion in the 1840s on the former site of the Pell manor house. Bartow descendants sold the mansion, its carriage house, and 200 acres to New York City in 1888. The city only takes care of the mansion's exterior, mows the front lawn, but provides no funds.

Funding is the domain of the International Garden Club, which has struggled for more than 70 years to manage and maintain the property. The club's focus is historical preservation, so most of the modest budget is spent on the mansion's interior and its mixture of nineteenth-century Empire furnishings, half on loan from city museums.

In recent years, the club's special project has been the restoration of the carriage house. By 1988 the club had raised half the $875,000 needed, unraveled miles of city red tape, and was ready to begin the physical work of the restoration.

BARTOW-PELL MANSION MUSEUM AND GARDENS, Shore Road, Pelham Bay Park, Bronx, NY 10464. (212) 885-1461. On the National Register of Historic Places.

OPEN
Mansion and grounds, Wednesday, Saturday, Sunday, noon to 4 P.M.; closed Thanksgiving weekend, Christmas, New Year's Day, and the last three weeks of August. Reservations can be made for group tours, Tuesday through Friday. Admission fee.

FACILITIES
· Arrangements can sometimes be made for luncheons for group tours.
· Mansion not accessible to people with physical disabilities; garden has limited accessibility, no paved paths.

EVENTS
· Christmas Boutique, one weekend in early December.
· Community Open House during Bronx Week, usually in May.

DIRECTIONS
Triborough Bridge to Bruckner Expressway (I-278) to Hutchinson River Parkway north. Take City Island/Orchard Beach exit. Go to traffic circle; take third turnoff on right (sign says to Split Rock and Pelham golf courses). Go ½ mile to stone pillars of Bartow-Pell on the right.

✤

BROOKLYN
BOTANIC GARDEN

BROOKLYN, NEW YORK

✤ Within its 52 acres, which is small as major botanical gardens go, the Brooklyn Botanic Garden is an educational tour de force, an outdoor classroom that includes 14 specialty gardens, linked like beads on a string along a man-made stream.

The gardens range from the pragmatic to the aesthetic, from displays of mulch beds to the most delicate pearl of all, the Japanese Hill-and-Pond Garden.

Comparative beds of flowers and shrubs are strung randomly along a stream. (Comparative beds are those in which many varieties of one species are planted together to compare such aspects as color, size, hardiness, and length of blooming period.)

Most of these beds are labeled. The gardens and rocks are labeled. Even the window boxes in the outdoor patio restaurant are labeled.

All this outdoor learning is bulwarked with a year-round educational program of seminars, classes, lectures, field trips, how-to handbooks, videotapes, and short documentaries on garden subjects.

With learning packed into every square inch, the Brooklyn Botanic Garden lives up to the directive of its founding fathers, who in 1910 made public education a priority. Such a priority was unusual in an era when most of the nation's newly established botanical gardens were pouring resources into research on the medicinal and food plants that would most benefit mankind.

Most tourists begin their visit at the prize garden that everybody rushes to see when the cherry blossoms are in bloom, the Japanese Hill-and-Pond Garden, built in 1914.

The garden incorporates elements from three religious traditions spanning 12 centuries: the garden as a holy place to lure gods from their river and mountain habitats (Shintoism); garden-as-paradise (Buddhism); and the garden as a retreat for meditation, for "centering" oneself, becoming one with every pebble and rock and thus one with the universe (Zen).

The Japanese garden is a symbolic idealization of nature, restrained in color and limited in plant selection. Paths wind through pines that look as if they were sculptured by the wind on a rocky seacoast. Junipers, hollies, and yews are pruned into cloud shapes, balls, and free-form groupings, layer upon layer, level upon level throughout the entire garden.

There are slashes of color—a flowering quince and tree peonies in spring, and a threadleaf maple, translucent ruby red in autumn.

But the most dominating color is that of a *torii*, a huge wooden construction painted Chinese red. In Japan the *torii* signifies that a temple is nearby. Placed offshore in the pond, the color impact of the *torii* is doubled by its reflection in the water.

Far less showy and far less frequented is a subtle garden tucked in a far corner of the property and known by the dowdy name of Local Flora Section. In this man-made environment, the nine ecological zones found within a 100-mile radius of New York City have been shoehorned into a delightful, secluded two acres. Rock formations, topography, water courses, the amount of light, and the acidity or alkalinity of the soil have been carefully manipulated so that the 100 species of native or

❦

PRECEDING PAGE: A *wooden* torii *painted Chinese red dominates the pond of the Japanese Hill-and-Pond Garden.*

naturalized plants that grow within these nine ecological zones can survive.

Shaded by red maples, oaks, and pines, dragonflies hum over a miniature bog. Golden-club dots an artificially created kettle hole 50 feet across. (Kettle holes, in their natural state, were created by a melting chunk of ice as glaciers receded some 10,000 years ago.) A tiny wet meadow is lush with frogs, mosses, jewelweed, and marsh marigolds. Blueberry, pitch pine, and holly grow in pine barrens the size of a backyard; goldenrod, milkweed, and asters, in a dry meadow. So on it goes through the nine zones.

Since few plants are labeled here, buy the small, excellent handbook, *Local Flora Section*, with drawings of plant life, at the bookstore before you begin your ramble.

Because of its fragility, the garden is only open weekdays and never to school groups.

Over a two-week period each spring, the Cherry Esplanade is second to none in a delicacy of changing pastels. A double row of Kwanzan cherry trees is canopied by a double row of tall, pruned Norwegian maples. The maples come into bloom with tiny, starlike lemon yellow flowers just as the cherry buds, wrapped in small, silky red cases, begin to spangle the cherry trees with polka dots. A week later, the red and yellow colors change. The maples begin to unfurl their dark burgundy leaves just as the cherry blossoms are beginning to explode into showers of deep pink.

Along the stream the comparative beds, though less dramatic, are highly instructive. There are beds of spirea and hydrangea. Low-lying junipers sprawl in free-form beds. In a hedge wheel, each of the 18 spokes is a different kind of hedging plant—boxwood, viburnum, standard orange, holly, yew, hemlock, cypress—so the home gardener can compare them for density, form, shape, and texture.

A bed of barberries was planted in the 1920s. Who can get excited about barberries? Barberries are thorny, commonplace habitués of public parks, planted to keep people in or out of an area. They are aggressive, invasive, hardy, and perform their job well with little maintenance.

In the barberry bed at Brooklyn Botanic Garden, 20 varieties reign in psychedelic splendor. There are yellow-green fountains of barberries dotted with tiny red buds; dusky eggplant-colored bushes sprinkled with fiery orange buds; carrot green bushes speckled with lime green buds. There are exotic barberries with a bamboolike structure, and some with blooms that look like yellow lilac clusters. Nearby on an island in the stream, the leaves of a dense stand of bamboo click in the wind.

Other individual gardens include a Shakespearean Garden; a Fragrance Garden; an Herb Garden that incorporates a crisp Elizabethan knot of crushed brick, coal, and marble chips that glitter within boxwood borders; a magnolia terrace; and an acre of roses, called the Cranford Rose Garden.

In the Osborne section a grand staircase leads to a broad promenade. Green lawns unroll between huge clipped green balls of shrubbery fringed with white flowers. A pair of fluted, freestanding columns, one Greek and the other Art Deco, mark each end of the promenade.

Three new conservatories opened in 1988, housing palms, ferns, succulents, cacti, and a new Sonoran Desert collection. The collection, including 3,300 pounds of cacti, was trucked from Arizona where a proposed federal canal and dam will drown thousands of other desert plants, many of them threatened or endangered species.

Incorporated within the new conservatory complex, the turn-of-the century Palm House has been restored to its original Victorian elegance and can be rented for private parties.

In the new conservatories, you can follow a trail of evolution that traces the origins and development of plant life throughout the millennia and see a collection of bonsai, 1,000 specimens, some a century old. Started in the 1920s, the collection is the largest in the country and looks impressive in its new Oriental setting in the Bonsai House.

While bonsai is now commonplace, even showing up at the posher Woolworths, this highly intricate art of dwarfing plants can take decades to complete. Cuttings or roots are first wired into place, often at an angle, then pinched of new growths. Limbs are wired to achieve balance and the desired geometric shape. The wires must be moved gently and often. The result is miniature "tray" gardens—forests of pines, bamboos, junipers, wisteria, even maples and elm, that become collectors' items.

Brooklyn Botanic Garden, located as it is in the heart of Brooklyn (population 2.3 million), is often impacted with people. Attendance runs to 20,000 on a spring weekend. Guards have multiplied with the attendance. They are everywhere—on foot and motorized. You may not picnic, wander off paths, go barefoot, or sit on the grass except in the Cherry Esplanade. Sad, but true. Such is the price of success—the education of such a large public, never foreseen by the garden's forefathers.

BROOKLYN BOTANIC GARDEN, 1000 Washington Avenue, Brooklyn, NY 11225. (212) 622-4433. Privately owned and partially supported by New York City.

OPEN
- General gardens, April through September, Tuesday through Friday, 8 A.M. to 6 P.M.; weekends and holidays, 10 A.M. to 6 P.M.; October through March, Tuesday through Friday, 8 A.M. to 4:30 P.M.; weekends and holidays, 10 A.M. to 5 P.M. The entire garden is closed on Mondays except when a public holiday falls on that day. No admission fee.
- Japanese Hill-and-Pond Garden, April through October, Tuesday through Sunday, 10 A.M. to 4 P.M. Admission fee on weekends and holidays.
- Cranford Rose Garden, June through October, Tuesday through Friday, 9 A.M. to 4:30 P.M.; Saturday, Sunday, and holidays, 10:30 A.M. to 4:30 P.M.
- Local Flora Section, mid-April through mid-October, Tuesday through Friday, 10:30 A.M. to 3:30 P.M. Free tour first Sunday of each month at 1 P.M.
- Plant and gift shop, Tuesday through Sunday, 10 A.M. to 5 P.M.
- Conservatories, Tuesday through Sunday, 10 A.M. to 5:30 P.M.

FACILITIES
- Outdoor Terrace Restaurant.
- Plant and gift shop.
- Herbarium (250,000 dried plant specimens).
- Horticultural Reference Library.
- Brooklyn Botanic Garden Research Center, Ossining, NY. (914) 941-8886. Includes 223 acres with wildflower, herb, and perennial gardens; 6 miles of hiking trails; educational programs.
- Clark Garden, Albertson, Long Island. (516) 621-7568. A 12-acre horticultural center with emphasis on home gardening.
- Free plant information service by mail and phone.
- Most of the gardens and conservatories are accessible to those with physical disabilities.

EVENTS
- Garden tours, mid-March through mid-November, weekends, 1 P.M. except for Memorial Day, Fourth of July, and Labor Day weekends. For groups, by prior arrangement only. No admission fee.
- Workshops, lectures, art exhibits, concerts, films on botanical and horticultural subjects, year-round. Some require admission fees.
- Classes on gardening, bonsai, flower arranging, arts, crafts, nature photography, landscaping; fall, winter, and spring. Admission fee.

- Children's garden programs, spring, summer, and fall. Admission fee.
- Annual Plant Benefit Sales, first Wednesday and Thursday in May; Election Day in November.
- Annual Fence Art Show and Sale, one Sunday in September and in June.
- Orchid sale, first Saturday in December and last Saturday in March.
- Cherry Blossom Weekend with Japanese poetry, music; last weekend in April.

DIRECTIONS
Traffic is horrendous. By subway, take the Lexington Avenue Express, Number 4 or 5, or the Seventh Avenue IRT Express, Number 2 or 3, to Eastern Parkway station (one stop after Grand Army Plaza). Or take the IND D or M train to Prospect Park station. If you must drive, there is a parking lot, shared by the garden and the Brooklyn Museum.

THE CLOISTERS

NEW YORK, NEW YORK

The Cloisters is not really a cloister at all, but bits and pieces of medieval abbeys and monasteries salvaged from Europe in the 1920s. Romanesque and Gothic arches, lintels, columns, and capitals were rescued from abandoned fields and private gardens and painstakingly reassembled on a magnificent overlook above the Hudson River.

The Cloisters is a compelling story of the vision and persistence of four men: sculptor George Grey Barnard, the original collector of the medieval architectural artifacts; architect Charles Collens; James J. Rorimer, a Metropolitan Museum curator who later became its director; and John D. Rockefeller, Jr., who had both the vision and money to build a museum of medieval art on a New York City hilltop.

Rockefeller bought Barnard's collection and the land that is now Fort Tryon Park, which includes the hilltop where the Cloisters stands.

Ultimately, he bought the bluffs across the Hudson from the Cloisters to assure that the view would never be interrupted by real estate development.

The efforts of these four men stretched over a decade and resulted in the Cloisters, a series of red-roofed structures that resembles a medieval cloister.

A branch of the Metropolitan Museum of Art, the Cloisters houses, among other things, the famous Unicorn Tapestries. In woolens and silk, the tapestries weave the tale of a unicorn, captured, slain, and resurrected. The allegory is depicted against a backdrop of life in the 1500s—detailed costumes, plants, animals, and architecture.

Incorporated within the Cloisters are four monastic-style gardens: the outdoor garden of the Bonnefont Cloisters; the Cuxa and Trie cloisters, both arcaded and open to the sky; and the interior Saint-Guilhem courtyard, enclosed by a skylight.

All four of these small, thoughtful gardens share elements of quietude. As the sun moves across the sky, the colors of their limestone walls—gold, pearly gray, and salmon pink—change in intensity. The reflected light bathes the gardens in a kind of luminosity. In each of these courtyards, the Cloisters' gardeners offer a movable feast. By season, they fill giant clay plots with myrtle, oleanders, jade plants, and waist-high rosemary. Then they periodically move and regroup them. Sometimes they build raised brick beds, sodding them with patches of grass.

The gentle drip of fountains, the scent of narcissus, grape hyacinths, dianthus, lilies, and the piped, sweetly thin recorded music of troubadours encourage contemplation, which after all is what monastic gardens were all about.

The Saint-Guilhem Cloister centers about a dark gray limestone fountain set on a gray textured floor of polished pebbles. In the diffuse light from the skylight, the limestone walls appear gray, their carved acanthus and grape leaves grayer still. How can this gray-upon-gray be so peaceful and reassuring? Then comes a single stab of color—a clay pot spilling over with ivies, dominated by a flowering quince or massed paper-white narcissus.

The Bonnefont Cloister garden, arcaded on two sides, looks south to a splendid but most unmedieval view of the George Washington

࿔

PRECEDING PAGE: *The garden of the Cuxa Cloister.*

12

Bridge. Symmetrical brick-edged beds are planted with 250 species of fruit trees, vegetables, and herbs common in the Middle Ages.

Space within a monastery garden was dear, so plants were highly utilitarian. There were vegetables and salad greens; herbs for cooking, for cosmetics, and for use as insect repellents. Monastic gardens were also the pharmacies of their day, so the Bonnefont garden includes medicinal herbs with such charming names as live-forever, feverfew, lungwort, throatwort, sneezewort, and birthwort (*wort*, from the Gothic *wourt*, meaning *used in combination with*).

One bed contains three dye plants of the primary colors that produced the myriad shades found in the Unicorn Tapestries. There is madder, for red; weld, for yellow; and woad, for blue. In the center is a twelfth-century wellhead, its rim grooved by the ropes that once drew forth thousands of buckets of water.

Below the south wall of the garden, a small crab apple orchard sends forth clouds of pink and white blossoms in spring.

The Cuxa Cloister garden is properly called a garth, an enclosed courtyard open to the sky. The garth is filled with grass squares and masses of flowers, a pleasure garden pretty to look at and pleasant to smell. Sloping red-tiled roofs overhang squat, dusty pink marble columns, enclosed in winter with glass panels. Then, fig trees, jasmine, and oleanders are set out in weathered wood tubs. Lime and lemon trees are moved indoors, as they were in medieval monasteries.

In a recessed fountain a spout of water pours from a lion's mouth. Originally purchased as a twelfth-century fountain of mottled red and cream marble quarried near Cuxa, the fountain turned out to be a fake. Its visual and aural impact does not suffer from this infidelity.

Crosswalks cut the garden into four grassy beds, each with a flowering tree—pear, quince, crab apple, and cornelian cherry that bears a small reddish yellow fruit in fall. In the corner of each grass plot, irises, asters, anemones, and Easter lilies grow, stalky and regal.

The Trie Cloister garden is a whimsy, incorporating as it does 50 of the 83 flowers identified in the Unicorn Tapestries. Among the lush tangle of garden flowers are wild strawberries, violets, primroses, carnations, bluebells, and lilies. They crowd about a 20-foot limestone fountain carved with saints and the Virgin and child. The seven "tapestry" trees are there too—hazelnut, oak, medlar, orange, pomegranate, and two kinds of holly.

By its sheer exuberance rather than by design, the garden somehow catches the spirit of the tapestries, particularly the seventh tapestry. In that one, the resurrected unicorn rests virtuously under a pomegranate tree, victorious over death.

THE CLOISTERS, Fort Tryon Park, New York, NY 10040. (212) 923-3700.

OPEN
March through October, Tuesday through Sunday, 9:30 A.M. to 5:15 P.M.; November through February, Tuesday through Sunday, 9:30 A.M. to 4:45 P.M. Closed Mondays, Thanksgiving, Christmas, New Year's Day. Admission donation.

FACILITIES
· Gift shop.
· Very limited access for people with physical disabilities.

EVENTS
· Tours every Tuesday, Wednesday, Thursday, 3 P.M.
· Special gallery workshops for families, afternoons during Easter and Christmas holidays. No admission fee.
· Gallery lectures, weekends.
· Concerts of medieval, early baroque, and renaissance music, Sunday afternoons, fall through spring; tickets by mail subscription only. Admission fee.

DIRECTIONS
Henry Hudson Parkway north to first exit after George Washington Bridge. By subway, IND Eighth Avenue A train to 190th Street–Overlook Terrace. After you get off the subway, take Number 4 bus or walk through Fort Tryon Park, a 15-minute walk with magnificent views of the Hudson River.

THE
CONSERVATORY
GARDEN

NEW YORK, NEW YORK

The Conservatory Garden—a jewel within a jewel—sits within six acres of Central Park. Originally laid out with WPA funds during the Depression, it was to be an estate garden for Everyman. And Everyman's garden it is today: the scene of summer weddings, fashion and television shoots, lovers wandering under the wisteria pergola, story telling by the lily pond.

But the real glory of the Conservatory Garden is its peace, 40 paces from the traffic roar of Fifth Avenue. Once you are through the gates and down a flight of stone stairs, the peace envelops you—the scent of lilacs, sage, and roses in season; the hum of bees in the crab apple blossoms; the quieting gray, green, and silver plantings set in orderly patterns against clipped boxwood and yew hedges. Fountains splash gently.

New Yorkers need calm, and calm the original Parks Department designers provided by sinking the garden 20 feet below street level. They divided this giant oval into three gardens, then ringed off the six acres by banks planted with wildflowers and flowering shrubs.

New Yorkers enter their garden through massive, forbidding gates that look as if, as Carl Sandburg once wrote, "only rain and death and tomorrow" could get over them. The gates were made in Paris in 1894 for the Vanderbilts' Fifth Avenue mansion. Decades later when Gertrude Vanderbilt Whitney donated the gates to the city, they were moved 40 blocks north and installed as the entrance to the garden.

The gates open onto the formal Center Garden, the middle of three sections. A green lawn unrolls between two crab apple allées, a magnificent glory of pink and white in spring. A fountain jets a single spout of water 30 feet into the air. The backdrop to this vista changes by season. A 50-year-old wisteria vine that twists over a semicircular iron pergola is bare-boned in winter, sprigged with purple clusters in spring, and becomes a canopy of gauzy green in summer.

The centerpiece of the North Garden is an oval pool with three bronze dancing nymphs, ringed with parterres of pink begonias, alternating with gray-green santolinas. Lamb's-ears, artemisia 'Silver Mound', and pale purple sage line flagstone walks. White mums sometimes escape their beds and spill onto a pathway. Half-century-old 'Silver Moon' roses hang from iron arches. Banks rising from the parterres blaze with 20,000 Darwin tulips in spring and with mums in fall. All this floral geometry is contained by a ruff of pink roses, spirea, and salmon-colored quince that runs around the outermost edge of the oval.

Quite different is the South Garden, intimate and charming in the English cottage garden tradition. Paths loop around horseshoe-shaped beds, unruly with tumbles of yarrow, purple smokebush, pink and yellow daylilies, flax, and butterfly bush. Benches are tucked alongside serpentine ilex hedges. Two bronze children, tarnished to a soft bottle green, gaze into a reflecting pool. This is the "Secret Garden," named after Frances Hodgson Burnett's classic story of two children who discover a long-deserted garden and bring it to life again.

All this garden magic was wrested in the 1970s from acres of broken glass, graffiti, and derelicts. "As unloved as a garden could be—a perfect mess," states the garden's present director, Lynden B. Miller. "The bones of the garden, its basic design, are superb. And

᪥

PRECEDING PAGE: *Two bronze children preside over the lily pool in the "Secret Garden," named after Frances Hodgson Burnett's classic children's story.*

those European gardeners who came here in the Depression from the Long Island North Shore estates—gardeners are always the first to be let go—knew what they were doing. But imagine, the garden went from fourteen full-time gardeners in 1937 to zero in 1970!"

On the brink of fiscal disaster in the mid-1970s, the city had other priorities. The garden fell into decay. The rebirth began when the New York Committee of the Garden Club of America raised funds to repair the fountains. A $50,000 gift from Rockefeller Center spurred the committee's efforts and provided basics. Workers dug four feet of leaf mold into flower beds, pruned the crab apple trees, wisteria, and lilac bushes, resodded the central green. Then the city, in concert with the private not-for-profit Central Park Conservancy, took over. This partnership operates the garden today.

Then in 1987, the miracle happened. In honor of their parents' sixtieth wedding anniversary, the Weiler-Arnow family, New York philanthropists, endowed the garden with a gift of $1.5 million. "It was the answer to our dream," said Lynden Miller.

Everyman's prices still prevail. Concerts are free. Weddings can be held in the garden for a small donation, and prices for professional photography shoots run well below commercial rates.

THE CONSERVATORY GARDEN, Central Park, Fifth Avenue at 105th Street, New York, NY. Operated jointly by New York City Department of Parks and Recreation and Central Park Conservancy. Mailing address: 830 Fifth Avenue, New York, NY 10031. (212) 360-8236 / 860-1330.

OPEN
Daily, 8 A.M. to dusk.

FACILITIES
Wheelchair access at northwest gate at 106th Street.

EVENTS
· Two free concerts in warm months.
· Group tours can be arranged by telephoning in advance.

DIRECTIONS
Fifth Avenue buses Numbers 1, M2, M3, and M4 run southbound; the same buses run north one block east on Madison Avenue. The nearest stop on the Lexington Avenue IRT subway line is the Number 6 train at 103rd Street.

❧

THE GARDEN
PEOPLE

NEW YORK, NEW YORK

❧ Amid roller skaters, dog walkers, skate boarders, and strollers, 40 volunteers called the Garden People work their magic along the concourse in Riverside Park. With the approval of the New York City Department of Parks, they have created what appears to be a grand old English perennial border.

On closer look, this mosaic of dappled color is 30 separate plots planted in as many styles and divided from each other by a few stones or bricks. Amazingly, the plots all fit together.

Barbara Stonecipher, treasurer of the group, explains. "Nobody says to his neighbor, 'I'm planting red. Are you planting blue?' It just works!"

Deep pink 'Betty Prior' roses back up against lavender malvas. In one plot, an arc of stepping-stones divides purple petunias and orange marigolds. In another, a large clump of Japanese irises shadows plum-colored corncockle that spreads onto the pavement.

The plots are arranged in two sections: a rectangle, 175 feet long, and an octagon, 40 feet across. The octagon is the communal garden where new volunteers begin working under the supervision of experienced gardeners until an individual plot opens up in the rectangle, an event that happens only two or three times a year.

The Garden People are also working on the hillside between the octagon and the West Side Highway, turning it into a wildflower meadow. They first planted wildflower seeds, then bulbs and perennials, like daffodils and daylilies, which will spread and hold their own against the invasive mugworts and grasses that grow along the highway.

Many of the group are sophisticated gardeners, their obsession with plants clear. Some examples in the octagon are *Geranium endressii* 'Wargrave Pink', *Salvia leucantha, Artemisia absinthium,* filipendula, caryopteris, santolina, *Centaurea macrocephala,* hyssop, Russian sage, *Brunnera macrophylla, Euonymus alata, Lychnis coronaria,* nigella, *Lysimachia clethroides,* and horseradish. "How nice to speak Latin with you this evening," says the gardener, discussing her plantings with a visitor.

The Garden People were bulldozed out of their first site on Broadway and 86th Street and settled in Riverside Park in 1982. Because the garden brings more people to the concourse—and a used park is a safe park—the Parks Department shares its toolshed with the gardeners, ties the garden into the city water supply, and has installed a wrought-iron fence around the garden to discourage dogs and flower-pickers.

The Garden People's rules are simple: no vegetables, no chemical pesticides, and $15 a year dues. Money for tools, plants, seeds, and fertilizer comes from contributions. A fishbowl set out by the garden nets as much as $200 on a good summer weekend.

THE GARDEN PEOPLE, Riverside Park (between 90th and 91st Streets, west of Riverside Drive), New York, NY.

OPEN
Always.

FACILITIES
· Picnicking permitted.
· Accessible to people with physical disabilities via the 91st Street path; no steps, but fairly steep.

DIRECTIONS
Paths enter the park at 89th and 91st streets off Riverside Drive. The Number 5 bus runs on Riverside Drive. The IRT subway Number 1 train stops on Broadway at 86th Street; Numbers 2 and 3 trains stop at 96th Street.

THE NEW YORK BOTANICAL GARDEN

BRONX, NEW YORK

The New York Botanical Garden is one of the foremost horticultural institutions in the world, a leader in botanical education, science, and ecology, and a paradise of plants. But to many New Yorkers, it is a grand extension of their backyard, or the only backyard they have—and, in friendly fashion, they treat it as their own. People stroll along the paths; lie on blankets sunbathing, reading the paper, or sleeping; crouch at flower level, getting a camera angle just right.

On 250 rolling acres, the Garden encompasses more than two dozen collections—among them, daffodils, oaks, magnolias, and conifers; a dozen special gardens; 40 acres of the only natural forest in New York City; and the famed symbol of the Garden, the Enid A. Haupt Conservatory.

The Conservatory is an extravaganza of glass modeled after

London's Crystal Palace. In summer, when most of the glass is whitewashed to protect plants from intense sun, it looks like a wedding cake. In the clear glass of winter, it is a translucent castle. Built at the turn of the century, the Conservatory was restored in 1978 and named for its major benefactress, Enid A. Haupt, philanthropist and former publisher and editor-in-chief of *Seventeen* magazine.

You approach the Conservatory through an elegant outdoor courtyard, between parterres of box and double allées of hornbeams clipped to a solid rectangle of foliage. On either side of the center court, twin reflecting pools are fringed with papyrus, cattails, and Egyptian lotus. The Conservatory's 11 connecting galleries, each a different, controlled environment, wrap around the pools and court.

The dome of the Palm Court soars 90 feet, seemingly into the clouds that can be seen racing by open panes of glass. Among the palms, a stand of bamboo rises as high as the glass dome. At the center of this splendid space, a sugar palm wafts 20-foot leaves over a pleasantly noisy fountain of three cast-iron maidens.

In the fern forest, a waterfall cascades down a mountain of volcanic rock. This gallery has its own "magical mystery tour"—a skywalk that climbs around the mountain, dodging baskets of hanging ferns. More ferns—staghorns—are silhouetted against the glass. Toward the end of winter, huge tubs of orchids are brought into the fern forest as they come into bloom, often 30 to 40 flowers on a single spike.

Two galleries, called "show houses" by the Garden staff, stage seven changing floral spectacles a year. Each is a tour de force that starts from scratch: new paving, watercourses, boxwood parterres changed, huge trees and shrubs installed. A staff committee and visiting specialists like the master of Kiku-Ka Ten, the traditional Japanese chrysanthemum display, plan the shows two years in advance.

In the main show house on a recent Mother's Day, a stream meandered through moss-covered banks planted with cream, blush, and lavender columbines and the palest of lavender irises. Five-foot mounds of marguerites looked sheared in their perfect roundness, and a carpet of pink-white-violet pansies edged a herringbone-brick path. Spiky foxgloves, spirea, moss phlox, and regal lilies smelled of spring. In the adjoining show house, another brick walk wound through hip-high masses of pink and white snapdragons, which alternated with double-

❧

PRECEDING PAGE: *The Enid A. Haupt Conservatory, reflected in one of the twin pools along its facade.*

flowered feverfew, white and lavender stock, blue salvia, and white azaleas.

The seven other Conservatory galleries exhibit cacti from North American deserts, plants from the deserts of southern Africa, tropical flora arranged according to their evolutionary development, rare orchids and carnivorous plants, baskets of flowering plants, changing displays of potted flowers, and a grocery store garden demonstrating the relationship between packaged foods and the plants they come from.

Outdoors, herb, perennial, tulip, and demonstration gardens spread out around the Conservatory. The Jane Watson Irwin Garden of perennials is laid out in a series of courtyards. In one, 60 clematis species, some with blooms as big as salad plates, twine over a wooden arbor. Wide paths, spacious open areas decorated with small crab apples in wooden box planters, and benches in sun and shade entice you to stop and ponder the orchestration of leaf and flower color, height, and texture. In one spring bed, shockingly bright euphorbia, forget-me-nots, and downy-leaved orange geums make a rousing combination.

A daffodil-daylily border presents a rare opportunity to compare many varieties in one place. For 300 feet along a path leading to the perennial garden, large clumps of individual daffodil cultivars, 124 in all, bloom over a three-week period in spring. (You may be perversely glad to see that the Garden's so-called pink daffodils are no closer to the clear pinks in the catalogs than the muddied colors in your own garden.) In summer, the show is repeated with 126 daylily cultivars planted alternately with the daffodils.

An encyclopedic display of tulips runs in blocks of knockout color along a 170-foot walk. From 100 to 200 bulbs of a single tulip are planted per block—first, a six-foot square of orange-red tulips; next, six feet of red-and-white-striped tulips; then, in succession, blocks of tulips in red, orange, yellow, black, pale yellow, heavy cream, yellow with red stripes.

The tulips are dug up the third week in May and donated to community gardens. If the leaves are allowed to wither naturally and the bulbs kept cool, some will bloom again the following year.

Annuals replace the tulips, and soon another visual hit explodes—blocks of rose nicotiana, blue ageratum, yellow daisies, red zinnias, white cleome, orange marigolds, and pink zinnias.

Unusual for demonstration gardens, the four here are designed for charm as well as horticultural ideas. Each small, contained garden is fenced in a different style. A split-rail fence encloses the Louise Loeb Vegetable Garden of widely spaced raised beds set in paving blocks. A rustic stone wall fronts the Rodney White Country Garden of native plants and wildflowers that thrive in sun and shade. Behind a curlicued iron fence and pergola, annuals and perennials in the Mae L. Wien Summer Garden provide mid- to late-summer color. Bricks and lattice-work fence Helen's Garden of fragrant plants—daphne, dianthus, lilies, roses, nepeta, sweet woodruff, and peonies. Three more demonstration gardens are in various planning stages.

A short hike from the Conservatory, the Thomas H. Everett Rock Garden fits snugly in a valley between natural rock outcroppings. This three-acre garden, unusually large for a rock garden, deserves many long visits—its horticultural variety and density are too much to assimilate at one time.

The feeling of density is intensified because the garden has lost its sense of depth and space over the years. Some plantings have grown out of balance. One azalea is now so big that you can't see the waterfall behind it. You might think at first that you are in a dwarf conifer garden, their presence is so strong. The conifers, azaleas, and other shrubs were meant to be the "permanent" elements that give structure to a garden and provide a background for herbaceous material. (*Herbaceous* describes any plant that does not have a woody stem or that seasonally dies back to the root system.) Overgrown and overbearing, they are being cut back and replanted to restore the balance.

Also being restored or repaired are the scree, the graveled bed that gives alpine plants the exacting drainage they need to survive; the bed of the stream that runs through the garden, so waterfalls will spill freely once again; and the watering system that emulates the constantly melting glacial ice conditions of a moraine.

In the Rock Garden, plants mix needle to leaf in constantly varying patterns of texture and color. Pieris, with drooping pale bells and dusky red new growth, perches above a stream edged with pink and white primulas. A small weeping hemlock and smaller Atlas cedar "drip" over a green carpet of *Epimedium grandiflorum* tinged with rose. In the middle of the garden, an open stretch of grass around the stream provides momentary breathing space amid the concentration of plantings.

The Rock Garden may look natural, but the late Thomas Everett, author of the renowned 10-volume *New York Botanical Garden Illustrated Encyclopedia of Horticulture,* created its rocky ledges and sheltered nooks in 1934. With a team of horses and help from WPA workers, he moved boulders from other parts of the Garden and imported tons of gravel. The garden cost $4,600. Today the price would be $1 million.

In the Native Plant Garden, plants indigenous to the northeastern United States—most of them natives within a hundred-mile radius of New York City—thrive in different natural habitats. A path winds between a wet meadow and a sandy pine barren where the pyxie-moss, turkeybeard, and rattlesnake-master grow. Across a stream, the path curves around a limestone outcropping and through a woodland collection of 170 species and varieties of ferns.

Two new native plant habitats are Hempstead Plains and a serpentine garden (a kind of rock, not a shape). The Plains includes plants that once bloomed on the largest prairie east of the Mississippi, located on western Long Island where the Nassau Coliseum now stands. The serpentine rock, imported from Staten Island, is very blue and green when wet and is high in magnesium. Certain plants, such as *Asclepias viridifolia,* have adapted so completely to serpentine conditions that they grow nowhere else.

In spring, the Native Plant Garden's wet meadow looks like a rather scruffy lawn. By mid-August, it has become a forest of Joe-Pye weed nine feet tall, goldenrod, asters, butterfly weed, and six-foot mallows with amazing seven-inch red flowers. This metamorphosis is achieved by mowing in late fall after the seeds have dropped and three times in spring before the end of May. Strips are cut in the last mowing so that the varying heights of the grasses and flowers undulate in waves when in full bloom.

The newest and most exciting construction at the Garden is the Peggy Rockefeller Rose Garden, laid out in 1988 as originally designed by landscape architect Beatrix Jones Farrand in 1915. An iron fence of alternating lattice and arches, painted green, surrounds the 2½-acre garden. Paths radiate from a central seven-sided gazebo, creating 70 rose beds. David Rockefeller donated $1 million for the rose garden in honor of his wife, Peggy, and the garden opened in September 1988 in time for their fortieth wedding anniversary. The rose bushes will number 5,000 when the collection is complete, a five-year task.

The main purpose of the Garden, since its founding in 1891, has been the study and protection of plants to improve human life. The keystone of the Garden's scientific activities is systematic botany—the discovery, classification, and evolutionary study of the world's plants. To date, only 5 percent of the world's one million plant species have been categorized. Beginning with the Garden's first field expedition to Puerto Rico in 1898, its scientists have traveled to every corner of the earth to collect plants. Most of the 800 expeditions have been to South America, where two-thirds of the world's plant species exist only in tropical rain forests. The collected plants are pressed, dried, and described in the Garden's Herbarium, one of the world's largest. Among its five million specimens are plants collected on Lewis and Clark's 1805 trek across the western United States.

Two institutes further the Garden's scientific research: The Institute of Ecosystem Studies at the Mary Flagler Cary Arboretum in Millbrook, New York (see page 68), and the Institute of Economic Botany (IEB), located at the Garden. The IEB's 16 scientists search for new plant sources for food, fuel, and medicine. Each year, for example, they send the National Cancer Institute 1,500 tropical plants to be tested as sources for possible anticancer and anti-AIDS agents. All plants produce chemicals as a defense against predators and in the process develop chemical compounds that scientists might never think of putting together in the laboratory.

The IEB is working on the *babassu* palm, which yields an oil that can fuel a car or cook a meal. Another find is the chameleonic *cocona*, or peach tomato, that is fruity in a sweet dessert, savory in salads or beef stew, good as a juice or sauce—and high in nutrition too.

The Garden also publishes more scientific literature—including nine journals, books, and floras (treatises on plants)—than any other botanical garden in the world.

A horticultural renaissance began at the Garden in 1985 with the hiring of a group of young horticulturists. They are slowly reinvigorating the gardens and restoring labor intensive collections like daylilies and irises that were largely ignored during the city's fiscal crisis. Currently, a major project is the dividing of the entire Garden into 100-meter grids to locate and inventory every plant. The information will be put into a computer that will eventually produce plant labels.

The Garden is raising $62.9 million to build a new Library and Plant Studies Center, scheduled to be completed in 1991, and to fund its second century as one of the world's great scientific, horticultural, and educational institutions.

THE NEW YORK BOTANICAL GARDEN, Bronx, NY 10458-5126. (212) 220-8700. The Garden is a private, not-for-profit corporation; buildings and grounds are owned by New York City.

OPEN
- Grounds, daily, April through October, 8 A.M. to 7 P.M.; November through March, 8 A.M. to 6 P.M. Voluntary admission fee; parking fee.
- Enid A. Haupt Conservatory, Tuesday through Sunday, 10 A.M. to 5 P.M., last admission at 4 P.M.; closed Mondays, Thanksgiving, Christmas, and New Year's Day. Admission fee, except free on Saturday, 10 A.M. to noon.
- Thomas H. Everett Rock Garden and Native Plant Garden, daily, April through October, 9 A.M. to 5 P.M. Admission fee.

- Library Reading Room, September through June, Monday through Thursday, 9:30 A.M. to 6 P.M.; Friday and Saturday, 9:30 A.M. to 4 P.M.; July and August, Monday through Friday, 9:30 A.M. to 4 P.M.

FACILITIES
- Snuff Mill River Terrace Café, open year-round, 9 A.M. to 5 P.M.
- Picnicking permitted in designated areas.
- Shop-in-the-Garden, daily, 10 A.M. to 5 P.M., located in the Museum building.
- Plant information by telephone, Monday through Friday, 10 A.M. to 3 P.M., (212) 220-8681.
- People with physical disabilities should address questions concerning access to security personnel at the Main Gate, the Enid A. Haupt Conservatory, and the Watson and Museum buildings.

EVENTS
- Bronx Artists' Guild Exhibit, June. No admission fee.
- Metropolitan Opera at NYBG, July. No admission fee.
- Riverside Shakespeare Festival, July-August. No admission fee; voluntary donation.
- Bronx Borough Senior Citizens Day, August. No admission fee.
- Holiday tree lighting ceremony, November. No admission fee.
- Guided tours through the grounds (seasonal) and Conservatory; call (212) 220-8747 for information about scheduled group tours.
- Education programs include graduate degrees offered in cooperation with New York colleges, courses ranging from botany to commercial flower arranging and nature photography, symposiums, and lectures. A catalog describing all programs is available at the Watson Building or by calling (212) 220-8747.

DIRECTIONS
By train, from Grand Central Station in Manhattan, Metro-North Harlem Line local to Botanical Garden station.

By car, Triborough Bridge to Bruckner Expressway east to Bronx River Parkway north. Take Botanical Garden exit to Southern (Kazimiroff) Boulevard, bear right, and continue to the Garden's Main Gate entrance on the left.

NEW YORK
CEMETERIES:
GREEN-WOOD AND
WOODLAWN

BROOKLYN AND BRONX,

NEW YORK

After John Lindsay was elected mayor of New York in 1966, he took a short flight over the city and commented ruefully that cemeteries were the largest and last green refuge within city limits. He was right, of course. In a city where real estate is king, even the late Robert Moses had trouble trying to move cemeteries. (They are immensely lucrative pieces of real estate in their own right.)

Two such green refuges are Brooklyn's Green-Wood Cemetery (1838) and Woodlawn in the Bronx (1863). Green-Wood's 478 gardenesque acres overlook five ponds, Upper New York Bay with glimpses of the Statue of Liberty, and warehouse terminals that line the Brooklyn waterfront.

Woodlawn is a leafy, sylvan retreat of 400 acres where the noisiest things are black crows and honking Canada geese. In this birders' paradise of 3,500 trees, ornithologists have spotted 119 species, from common nuthatches to rare Eastern kingbirds and yellow-bellied flycatchers.

The cemeteries share a unique niche in the history of landscape design. In the early 1800s, Boston's city fathers established the first burial grounds outside of town, creating cemeteries that looked like pastoral English hunting parks. They unwittingly started the American rural cemetery movement. These cemeteries became the forerunners of the great urban parks built during the last half of the nineteenth century. As such, Green-Wood was a working model for landscape designer Frederick Law Olmsted when he was designing Central Park.

Both are spectacles in the best beaux arts tradition, a felicitous combination of sculpture, architecture, and landscape. These are the reasons to visit Green-Wood and Woodlawn.

On a Sunday in spring in the 1850s, some 10,000 visitors would stroll Green-Wood's flower-spangled hills. They are still flower spangled, and spring is the best time to visit.

In each cemetery, daffodils, grape hyacinths, lilies-of-the-valley, and violets nestle at the base of marble urns, obelisks, and tombstones that look like knocked-off church spires set gently down on green lawns. There are masses of weeping everything: weeping willows, weeping beeches, weeping cherries. What doesn't weep, droops, dangles, or entwines: wisteria, golden-rain trees, spirea, honeysuckle, forsythia, and Virginia creeper. Ivy girdles Greek columns, miniature Gothic chapels, and limestone temples mounted with winged angels.

Stone maidens weep from the tops of pedestals and sarcophagi. They pray, kneel, fall prostrate over granite crosses. They hold laurel wreaths aloft; clutch lutes, prayer books, long-stemmed roses, and scrolls. They cradle children. But in the combined 878 acres of the two cemeteries, not one male allegorical statue can be found; not one David, not one Atlas. It is as if the female figure had cornered the Victorian grief market.

When you drive through the giant brownstone neo-Gothic gates at Green-Wood, you expect to see the angel Gabriel light upon the highest spire and blow his trumpet. Twenty-two miles of roads and thirty miles of paths with names like Sylvan Cliffs, Sycamore Grove, and Dewy Path weave among Chinese empress trees, brought to New York in the China clipper trade in the 1850s; sequoias from California, magnificent stands of horse chestnuts, and Brooklyn's own, the lowly ailanthus tree, scourged as a tenement dweller.

Tombstones, like everything else, have their fashions. At Wood-lawn in the first quarter of the twentieth century, a trunk-and-boulder style came into vogue. On huge tree trunks made of cast concrete, the names "mama," "poppa," and "uncle" are carved where each sawed-off limb is severed from the trunk. Clustering around each trunk is a family of flat-topped stumps close to the ground, each inscribed with the name and date of death of the deceased family member.

Other tombstones of cast concrete are fashioned to look like boulders. Some are 10 feet high and 5 feet across and are adorned with palm fronds and twiglike letters, also of cast concrete. On one, a child's sailor hat has been flung across the fake boulder, its concrete ribbons fluttering to the base. It is the grave of a 12-year-old, "Our Roberta."

Woodlawn bills itself as the final resting place of the famous. George M. Cohan, Victor Herbert, and Oscar Hammerstein are buried here. Herman Melville is buried under a stone quill and scroll. Mayor Fiorello La Guardia, New York's pugnacious "Little Flower," has, yes, a single flower carved into his tombstone.

After the unveiling of Queen Victoria's excessive gingerbread memorial to her beloved Prince Albert, William Gladstone, her prime minister, wrote, "Show me the manner in which a nation cares for its dead, and I will measure with mathematical exactness the tender sympathies of its people."

Green-Wood and Woodlawn measure those sympathies.

THE GREEN-WOOD CEMETERY, Fifth Avenue at 25th Street, Brooklyn, NY 11232. (718) 768-7300.

OPEN
Daily, 8 A.M. to 4 P.M. No admission fee but a pass is required of all visitors, obtainable at the superintendent's office at the main gate.

FACILITIES
Accessible to people with physical disabilities.

DIRECTIONS
West Side Highway or FDR Drive south to the Brooklyn Battery Tunnel. Stay on the right, exiting immediately at Hamilton Avenue. Take Hamilton Avenue about 4 or 5 blocks, cross a bridge, and turn right onto Third Avenue. Go about 2 miles, then turn left onto 25th Street. Go 2 blocks to Fifth Avenue. You truly cannot miss the gate.

THE WOODLAWN CEMETERY AND MAUSOLEUMS, Webster Avenue and 233d Street, Bronx, NY 10470. (212) 920-0500.

OPEN
Daily, 9:15 A.M. to 4 P.M., except when road conditions are hazardous.

FACILITIES
Accessible to people with physical disabilities.

EVENTS
- Concerts and dramas, one Sunday afternoon in February, March, April, May, and June in Woolworth Chapel, near Jerome Avenue gate.
- Memorial Day Concert, Sunday, outdoors under tent.
- George M. Cohan concert, Fourth of July afternoon, under weeping silver linden tree.

DIRECTIONS
Henry Hudson Parkway north, exiting at Mosholu Parkway to Jerome Avenue. Turn left at Jerome (north) and go about 25 blocks to 233d Street. Or take the Lexington Avenue or Seventh Avenue IRT uptown to the last subway stop, Woodlawn, about a 40-minute trip from midtown Manhattan.

❧

QUEENS BOTANICAL GARDEN

FLUSHING, NEW YORK

❧ Getting there is half the fun. From the subway you walk half a mile through an Oriental market district: Indian sari shops, exotic spice shops, and Korean food markets displaying translucent green vegetables and mauve-colored herbs that hang in bunches from overhead poles. A Chinese version of Woolworth's sells cakes imported from San Francisco, Thermos jugs and tinware from Hong Kong decorated with 1920s designs of flowers and checks, and a dazzling array of ceramics.

You are thus prepared for the fact that Flushing, a major business section of the borough of Queens, is now about 40 percent Asian. Most of the residents are young married couples and families on small incomes. They mix with Jewish senior citizens who reared their families in Queens 30 years ago, and with Italian-American and black families, mostly middle-class.

To serve this local ethnic constituency has always been the goal of the Queens Botanical Garden, a goal it fulfills inventively on a low budget—low relative to those of two of New York City's most prestigious botanical gardens, the New York Botanical and the Brooklyn Botanic Garden.

Within 16 acres the Queens Botanical Garden has amassed splashy concentrations of annuals and special interest gardens along asphalt paths, important for mothers with strollers and senior citizens.

At the entrance is a fine example of Victorian carpet bedding—showy rings of pink, coral, and white begonias, and dusty miller around an oval berm, crowned with a cycad. The same colors and flowers are repeated in flower beds that border a central promenade of oaks.

Five thousand rosebushes are planted in the Charles N. Perkins Memorial Rose Garden, originally donated by Jackson & Perkins Company, founded by Charles N. Perkins and one of the major purveyors of rose stock in the United States. The firm continues to supply the garden with new roses and tests new varieties here. The 1½-acre rose garden includes hybrid teas; floribundas that bloom all summer long; and grandifloras, a cross between the two, that sometimes reach a height of eight feet.

For home gardeners Backyards Gardens is a series of small zigzag-shaped plots that display the low-cost and low-maintenance plantings possible in patios and small backyards. Originally designed by local Long Island nurseries, the gardens include a pergola garden of ivies, hostas, and shade flowers; a rock garden of dwarf conifers, rock spray, and ornamental grasses; and a patio garden where pyracanthus, hydrangeas, and honey locusts grow in filtered sunlight.

Most popular of all in this community where large private gardens are a rarity is the Victorian Wedding Garden. Within a white picket fence camera-ready flower beds bloom with a calico of color from May to October. Tulips, lilies-of-the-valley, lilacs, and peonies give way to daisies, zinnias, marigolds, phlox, foxgloves, cosmos, asters, black-eyed Susans, and chrysanthemums.

A white wooden bridge spans a tiny stream. Bridal couples can be married in a Victorian gazebo, photographed in an old-fashioned swing for $50 for a half hour; or hold a reception in the garden for $245 per hour. Onlookers adore the celebrations—for free.

Other small specialty gardens include a Bee Garden, Bird Garden, All-American Garden of Vegetables and Flowers, Herb Garden, Flowering Cherry Tree Circle, Wildflower Walk, and forest.

Adjacent to these postage stamp gardens is a 16-acre orchard of crab apple and cherry trees, slated to become Gardens of the Orient; an Italian Mediterranean Garden with a conservatory; and a historical replica of one of the first commercial nurseries in this country, established by the Prince family under a royal charter granted by King George III. The Princes propagated plants from specimens they purchased from sea captains, who brought them home from their voyages around the world. The Princes then sold them to customers, among them George Washington, then developing his gardens and nurseries at Mt. Vernon.

QUEENS BOTANICAL GARDEN, 43-50 Main Street, Flushing, NY 11355. (718) 886-3800.

OPEN

Garden, daily, 9 A.M. to dusk. No admission fee.

Greenhouse, plant and gift shop, Monday through Friday, 10 A.M. to 4 P.M.; Saturday and Sunday, 9 A.M. to 5 P.M.

FACILITIES

- Food vending machines.
- Picnicking permitted in arboretum only.
- Plant and gift shop.
- Garden fully accessible to wheelchairs.

EVENTS

- Year-round program of children's tours and workshops; horticultural and vocational training classes for the mentally and physically handicapped by arrangement.
- Classes, workshops on gardening topics.
- Halloween program.
- Herb Fair, first Sunday in October.
- Apple and birdseed sale, last weekend in October.

DIRECTIONS

From Grand Central Station in Manhattan, take the subway, Number 7 train, Queens Line, to last stop, Main Street. The trip takes about 45 minutes. Walk south on Main Street about 7 blocks to garden entrance.

UNTERMYER
PARK AND
GARDENS

YONKERS, NEW YORK

Entering the Grecian Gardens of Untermyer Park is like stumbling across the remains of an old civilization in the middle of Yonkers. Buff-colored brick walls enclose three sides of this single large garden, designed in beaux arts style with fountains, water channels, and pools; sphinxes on top of double-column pedestals; and miles of marble mosaics. A Greek temple stands on the open side, a perfect aerie from which to view the Hudson River far below.

The garden, restored in 1979 for $2.5 million, has an abandoned, unused feeling. Life is missing because the fountains, channels, and pools are dry.

Flower beds planted with the usual municipal-garden annuals—ageratum, marigolds, dusty miller—border the dry water channels and gravel paths that bisect the length and width of the garden. Small conifers line the paths like so many dark green polka dots.

Just inside the entrance through an impressive Assyrian-style portal, you are brought up short by one of the funniest—and worst—bits of landscape planning imaginable. Two large weeping beeches have been given a blunt haircut to open up a partial view of the garden beyond.

Despite its oddities and unfulfilled promises, this football-field-sized garden creates a sense of wonder and discovery at finding such a classic landscape. Its grand scale and mosaic-decorated and ordered formality are of a style rarely seen today.

UNTERMYER PARK AND GARDENS, North Broadway, Yonkers, NY 10701. (914) 964-3500 (Yonkers Bureau of Parks, Recreation, and Conservation).

OPEN
Daily, sunrise to sunset.

FACILITIES
· Picnicking permitted.
· Gravel paths; accessible to people with physical disabilities.

EVENTS
· Performing Arts Festival (varied fare, opera to jazz), some Saturday nights in July and August, 8 P.M. No admission fee.
· Sunday afternoon concerts, June and July, 2 P.M. No admission fee.

DIRECTIONS
Henry Hudson Parkway to Saw Mill River Parkway to Executive Boulevard. Turn left onto Executive Boulevard and go to North Broadway. Turn left onto North Broadway, and Untermyer is 2 blocks ahead on the right, next to St. John's Hospital.

✿ WAVE HILL

BRONX, NEW YORK

✿ If you want to see the best old-fashioned flower garden in the East, Wave Hill is the place. That is only one of the gardens, breathtaking in abundance and imagination, that stretch along a bluff above the Hudson River at Wave Hill. Amid serene lawns and majestic trees, an herb garden, dry garden, alpine house, wild garden, monocot and aquatic gardens, and pocket plantings around the estate's two manor houses captivate both professional and amateur plantspeople.

What makes Wave Hill so special is the vision of Director of Horticulture Marco Polo Stufano: more plants to the square inch, more varieties, more new plant introductions. And all set within 13 cultivated acres, a size accessible to one's feet and not overwhelming to the senses.

Stufano is educator, artist, sleuth. "Our job is to stretch people's minds, to show how plants go together to make a garden. Doing a large garden or arranging furniture in a room, the same principles apply—the massing of forms and textures to get the look you want. We set out sticks and bushel baskets the size of a plant we want to use. Then we look at it for a while, move things around, and look some more."

Stufano and his eight-member staff constantly search for new plants. Most they grow from seed. They comb seed lists of American and English companies, of horticulture and rock garden societies. "The survival rate with English seeds is hit-or-miss," comments Stufano. "We just keep trying." They scrutinize the classifieds in gardening magazines. They trade with other public gardens. And sometimes a friend comes by with a new plant. Like *Cosmos atrosanguineus,* a dark, dark red flower with a chocolate smell, dropped off one day by a gardener from Connecticut.

Visitors will not be able to find at their local nursery many of the plants they see at Wave Hill. Stufano likes it that way. "It's less interesting if we keep to things everyone can do."

Nor will they find the same plants from one visit to the next. "The essence of a garden is change," Stufano says, "so I don't mind if a plant's flowering is short. An oriental poppy is grand one moment, gone the next."

He also doesn't worry about low or high maintenance. It should be kept within bounds, but interesting gardening is not easy, he asserts. There are, however, immediate rewards. "I love weeding," Stufano says. "It's dirty—and then it's clean."

The heart of Wave Hill is the 70-by-90-foot old-fashioned flower garden, masterminded by the late John Nally, who was Curator of the Gardens. Brick paths form eight large central beds and narrow beds around the perimeter. In the center, a raised circle displays weekly specials from the greenhouse. A rustic fence borders the garden on three sides—the greenhouse makes the fourth—offering support to climbing roses, clematis, and floppy stands of tall asters.

The layout of the flower garden is orderly and balanced, the plantings voluptuous and lush. Nally, trained as a printmaker, painted with plants, contrasting size, texture, and color. Huge perennials, some as big as shrubs, are set in carpets of ajugas and other ground covers that creep onto the brick paths. A five-foot cloud of delicate meadow rue,

⤳

PRECEDING PAGE: *The old-fashioned flower garden, with a clematis-covered tripod.*

37

topped by tiny lavender flowers, floats next to the dark green foliage of astilbe. Soft, furry artemisia is companion to spiky iris leaves. Abundant gray- and silver-leaved plants—stachys, Russian sage, three varieties of nepeta—rest the eye between onslaughts of color: blackish maroon dahlias, the dark red leaves and red flower of *Lobelia fulgens* 'Queen Victoria', and heliotrope.

The greenhouse is at its best beginning in February when the 10-foot acacia, bought years ago for $1.35, begins to flower. Pots of flowers are grouped and regrouped in the small entrance area in blazing combinations. On a day in May there might be intense masses of purple and orange—lobelia, nasturtiums, mimulus, larkspur, salpiglossis, and several varieties of osteospermum. In the background, a bougainvillea vine splashes its brilliant peachy orange and gold flowers up to the roof. By June the drama has moved outdoors.

Extravagance in the greenhouse, miniature marvels in the alpine house. Here, in a fitting space the size of a one-room schoolhouse, a rare group of small-scale alpine treasures thrive, the only collection of its kind in the Northeast. Because the small size of the alpine plants is too tempting to thieves, the plants can only be viewed through a window that runs the length of the house. Tables at eye level are crowded with pots of lewisias and gentians, drabas and primulas, and dozens more. Tiny pink and white flowers rise on stems no thicker than a pencil line, hovering 10 inches above their 1½-inch-tall clay pot. Foliage comes in many forms—basal rosettes, mossy mounds, furry, fernlike, or sharply bladed. Each plant is exquisite and perfect.

The wild garden is a garden of plants provided by nature, collected from all over the world, not a cultivated variety among them. The garden alters quickly as plants bloom and fade. If you don't go often, you are sure to miss something wonderful. Densely planted with flowers and shrubs, the wild garden looks like a highly textured hooked rug. Gravel paths meander among the irregularly shaped beds, past yews carved into shapes like giant green buffalo. The garden slopes gently upward to a six-sided summerhouse where people read in wooden lawn chairs, taking advantage of the breeze that blows on even the hottest day.

In the wild garden in spring, deep blue forget-me-nots mix with purple allium and chartreuse euphorbia. A clump of variegated Solomon's-seal sits under a shadbush next to white bleeding hearts. Arabis and snow-in-summer smudge the outline of the paths. Soft orange Icelandic poppies are scattered among red-purple cranesbill geraniums and great stands of purple, lavender, and white irises. In the middle, the twisted limbs of a cutleaf staghorn sumac curve out like a mad candelabrum.

Interspersed with the "formal" gardens are lilac and viburnum borders, a bed of annuals in unusual combinations that change each year, long perennial borders, a shade border, and an arbor of vines. Fifteen acres of woodlands complete the grounds.

Like most nineteeth-century Hudson River estates, Wave Hill was built as a summer home, within an easy train ride of New York City. In 1960 it was given to the city by the Perkins-Freeman family. Since 1967, Stufano has been working his horticultural alchemy so that Wave Hill will look like an old estate, not an institution. He has succeeded. Still Stufano says, "A garden is never right. You always hope that *next* year it will be right." Wave Hill is right, right now.

WAVE HILL, 675 West 252d Street, Bronx, NY 10471. (212) 549-2055.

OPEN
· Garden, daily, Memorial Day through Labor Day, 10 A.M. to 5:30 P.M., Wednesday till dusk, Sunday till 7 P.M.; other seasons, 10 A.M. to 4:30 P.M. Admission fee only on weekends.
· Greenhouse, 10 A.M. to 12 noon and 2 P.M. to 4 P.M.
· Gift shop, daily, 12 noon to 4:30 P.M.

FACILITIES
· Gift shop.
· Accessible to people with physical disabilities.

EVENTS
· Maple Sugar Festival, March.
· Bird walks and woodland walks, spring. No extra admission fee.
· Hudson River Day, June, workshops, walks, ongoing demonstrations about the Hudson River.
· Folk Day, July, folk music, workshops, concert.
· Summer sings.
· Outdoor dance performances, June and July.
· Annual bulb sale, October weekend. Gate admission credited toward purchase.
· Christmas bird count, Sunday in December, an identification field trip. No admission fee.
· Concerts, classical, from November through May. Admission fee.
· Winter Solstice Celebration, December, dance, song, drama for the whole family.
· Art exhibitions, indoor and outdoor, changing.

- Greenhouse and garden walks, every Sunday, 2:15 P.M. No extra admission fee.
- Toscanini on tape, concerts throughout the year.
- No extra admission fee for weekend events unless noted.

DIRECTIONS

By car, Henry Hudson Parkway to 246th–250th Street Exit. Continue north to 252d Street and turn left onto the overpass across the parkway. Go left at the stop sign and left again at the light. Proceed to 249th Street and turn right. Follow the road until it ends at the Wave Hill Gate.

By subway and bus (and a 7-minute walk), take the Broadway-Van Cortlandt Park subway line to 231st Street Station. Take the Bx 10 or Bx 7 bus at the northwest corner of 231st Street and Broadway. Get off at 252d Street. Walk across the parkway overpass and turn left. Walk to 249th Street and turn right. Follow the road until it ends at the Wave Hill Gate.

❦

THE JOHN P. HUMES JAPANESE STROLL GARDEN

LOCUST VALLEY, NEW YORK

❧ Can there be 100 shades of green? If so, they can be found in this Japanese woodland garden, which opened to the public in 1985.

The garden is subtle and small. Four hilly acres are planted under an umbrella of full-grown maples, oaks, and tulip trees. Subtle, because colors are of limited palette. Inky blacks blend into forest green, which fades into pale lemon, which melts into beige, then icicle white.

The garden is quiet. Paths curve, then disappear behind a stand of bamboo before reemerging upon tiny terraces of crushed white stone. Below in a ravine, a teahouse beckons.

The delicate sound of water soothes. A slender rivulet drops from a bamboo pipe into a black tufa basin before purling its way downhill over mossy rocks.

In the shattered sunlight, rich patterns and textures begin to emerge. The shagged leaves of a green Japanese threadleaf maple crinkle against the stubby branches of a smokey blue spruce. The black striated trunk of a locust shoots up 80 feet before disappearing into a green dome. A mote of sunlight catches the filigree lace of a cypress leaf, changing it to a translucent peach color. A cinnamon brown log is fringed with a collar of ivy.

In the garden the use of bamboo is elevated to an art form. The colors of the bamboo range from cactus green to saffron, circumference from matchstick to sewer pipe. Pieces of bamboo in different sizes are lashed together to make a fence, a gate, a frame for a wisteria pergola. The teahouse is a delicate structure of bamboo walls and shake roof banded by bamboo poles.

Black river stones are imbedded in stair steps of sparkling white quartz chips. The black stones zigzag across the steps, uneven in spacing. You cannot hurry. The stones impose their own discipline, dictating speed and view. Submission to the steps slowly turns to acceptance, then to recognition that this garden is a highly disciplined art form.

According to Zen tradition, a garden represents both nature and a journey through life. Yin/yang is the balance of opposites. Yin, the plants, are the flesh of the garden, and yang, the stones or skeleton. Water symbolizes blood. The paths are life's meandering search for inner peace, ultimately found in a symbolic sea or pond.

In the Japanese Stroll Garden, the teahouse overlooks the pond, a flat black disk of water that reflects a willow and black pines. Overhead, an oval disk of blue sky pierces the dome of greenery.

In Japan, this woodland garden would be found only in the homes of the very rich, land being so dear. On Long Island, the garden is the result of a dream and partnership between John P. Humes and his Japanese gardener, Douglas DeFaya. For 10 years the partnership flourished. Then Mr. Humes left for Austria, where he was ambassador for 10 years, and the garden fell into disrepair. In 1981, when Mr. Humes returned, he donated the garden to the North Shore Wildlife Sanctuary and hired Stephen A. Morrell, a graduate of the School of Horticulture of the New York Botanical Garden, to revitalize and manage the garden.

Since then, both Mr. Humes and Mr. DeFaya have died, and the garden has been opened to the public. In true Zen tradition, the garden struggles between opposites: the need for public support and the need to protect its fragility from overuse.

᠕

PRECEDING PAGE: *Stepping stones dappled with sunlight.*

THE JOHN P. HUMES JAPANESE STROLL GARDEN, PO Box 671, Locust Valley, NY 11560. (516) 676-4486.

OPEN
April 15 through October 31, Thursday, Saturday, and Sunday, 10 A.M. to 4 P.M. For nonmembers, by appointment only. Group tours by appointment only (with or without a tea ceremony demonstration), Thursday and Saturday. Admission fee.

FACILITIES
Not accessible to people with physical disabilities.

EVENTS
· Three annual exhibitions: bonsai in spring; chrysanthemums in fall; and each summer, a different aspect of Japanese culture, such as brush painting, bamboo and its uses. Admission fee.
· Workshops: Japanese arts, such as garden design, flower arranging, poetry, meditation; spring, summer, and fall. Admission fee.

DIRECTIONS
Queens Midtown Tunnel to Long Island Expressway to Exit 41 north to Route 107 north. Turn right at Wheatley Road (at the Upper Brookville police station). Cross over Route 25A. Wheatley Road becomes Wolver Hollow Road. Drive to end; turn right onto Chicken Valley Road. You will pass Planting Fields on your right. Drive 1.9 miles to Dogwood Lane. Turn right and make another immediate right into the parking lot.

OLD WESTBURY GARDENS

OLD WESTBURY, NEW YORK

The entrance into Westbury is breathtaking. A narrow road runs through a deep green gorge of beech trees, two double rows 90 feet tall. The road curves ever so slightly, vanishing into a wall of green. Only a pencil slit of sky overhead interrupts the flow. You don't want it ever to end. But it does, ridiculously. In the parking lot.

So park your car and return on foot to walk through these leafy cathedrals turned chartreuse chiffon in the filtered sunlight.

The smell of decaying leaves rises from the ground. A rooster crows in the distance. Time is suspended.

Then return to the twentieth century to tour Westbury, premiere garden of Long Island: 100 acres of landscaped vistas, meandering woodland paths, starched, parterred promenades, formal gardens, boxwood hedges, secret hideaways, ponds, and a wildflower garden.

The Westbury you see today is much as it was when originally laid out for Margarita "Dita" Grace Phipps, a beautiful English heiress and mother of four, who reigned as mistress over Westbury for 50 years.

Highborn, she was presented to Queen Victoria in 1894. An immensely rich American, John S. Phipps, sought her hand. Four years later, when she accepted, he promised her her heart's desire, an eighteenth-century Stuart-style mansion, reminiscent of the country seats where she had spent idyllic childhood summers. It was Westbury.

"What I want and what I have always asked for is an inexpensive little country home," Jay Phipps wrote his architect, Londoner George Crawley, when Westbury was under construction. But he spared nothing for his 27-year-old bride. Crawley, who had been commissioned to design the house, interiors, and gardens, hired English craftsmen, stone masons, and roofers. He imported antiques, wall panelings, and eight-foot-tall linden trees from Europe. A great lawn, hills, and ponds were carved from the flat farmland. Land was contoured to conceal two polo fields, a tennis court, and golf course.

In record time with record money (three years at a cost estimated between $15 and $20 million), the 72-room mansion was completed and fitted out with the required 125 servants.

As Peggie Phipps Boegner, daughter of Dita and Jay, commented years later, "[With Westbury] the Gold Coast was underway." Between 1900 and 1925, some 300 estates were built along the North Shore. Sixteen remain, six open to the public. Westbury's gardens are the most splendid.

Here are some of the highlights:

The Italianate Walled Garden is two acres of glory. Ropes of roses divide the garden into four sections, each a mirror image of the plot on the opposite side. Chinese dogwood, climbing hydrangeas, and bull bay magnolias are espaliered along one brick wall. Graveled paths run along 50-foot borders of lilies, irises, peonies, zinnias, asters, mums, daisies, dahlias—an unending spectrum of color, bees, and butterflies from the last frost in spring to the first frost in autumn.

Dita's favorite flowers—all white—encircle a Florentine limestone fountain. In spring, there are late-blooming Triumphator tulips, peonies, and alyssum; in summer, Japanese irises, spider flowers, phlox, and roses; and in fall, Snow Queen dahlias with stalky shasta daisies as a backdrop.

Italian cypress does not take kindly to Long Island's humidity and

❧

Preceding Page: *Dita Phipps's beloved Italian-style Walled Garden.*

45

frosts, so eastern cedars were planted in the corners instead. Trimmed, they manage to lend the same kind of romantic grandeur to the garden as a cypress does to an Italian landscape.

At the far end of the garden, a pergola of faintly chinoiserie persuasion is painted sea-foam green. Entwined with wisteria, the pergola girdles a lotus pond. White Siberian lilies, mint green grasses, and a ruching of chartreuse green lady's-mantle ring the edge. The green is a welcome respite from the intense colors of the rest of the garden.

In plan, the saucer-shaped Rose Garden looks like an Oriental rug, but in fact it more resembles a Victorian cabbage rose carpet in full bloom. Velvet ridges of moss squeeze out between the bricks, emphasizing the pattern of concentric circles. Dwarf Japanese hollies ring each rose-laden parterre. Red and white climbers cascade from the log pergola overhead.

For her eighth birthday, Dita's daughter, Peggie, received a diminutive thatch-roofed English cottage with a garden. Dainty pink ramblers, marigolds, lilies, foxgloves, delphiniums, sunflowers, yarrows, and daisies are massed in a jumble within a white picket fence. Tea sets and teddy bears sit on a rag rug in the cottage, now awaiting playmates that never come.

The Ghost Walk is a promenade of brooding hemlocks, similar to one Dita remembered from her childhood. It leads to the Peacock Room, named for two oxidized copper pots shaped and planted to look like peacocks. Blue lobelia forms the wings and clipped yew the long trailing cock feathers. The two peacocks strut in this small space, a cylinder 10 feet in diameter with hemlock walls 15 feet high. If there were a bench here, it would be a pleasant place to sit and contemplate the ring of blue sky overhead.

New as things go at Westbury are the wildflower meadow and demonstration gardens, the latter designed and paid for by *House and Garden* magazine in 1968. The purpose of the demonstration gardens is to show suburban gardeners what they can do in their own backyards without a Phipps fortune. There is a Gray Garden, a Green Garden, and a garden done in the "Japanese manner." Each garden is posted with labeled planting diagrams. The most interesting of these demonstration gardens is a 40-by-20-foot vegetable plot of raised beds. In this small space, an impressive summer-long array of fruits and vegetables is grown: lettuce, asparagus, beans, rhubarb, tomatoes, squash, and raspberries. The raised beds—a method used for centuries in France—are in part responsible for such a rich harvest in a small space. Raised beds drain better, are more easily fertilized, and retain moisture longer after watering.

For the record, Westbury Gardens includes a lilac walk, a pinetum, a bluebell walk, a boxwood garden, and a woodland trail around a lake, where a Temple of Love reflects in the still waters. All this is in impeccable taste, perfectly maintained.

OLD WESTBURY GARDENS, PO Box 430, Old Westbury, NY 11568. (516) 333-0048.

OPEN
· House and gardens, May through October, Wednesday through Sunday, 10 A.M. to 5 P.M., including holidays. Admission fee.
· Gardens, pre- and postseason for several weekends in April and November, when weather permits. Call in advance for confirmation.

FACILITIES
· Snack Bar in the Woods, 11 A.M. to 4 P.M., weather permitting.
· Picnicking permitted.
· Gift shop, 11 A.M. to 5 P.M.
· House and gardens accessible to people with physical disabilities.

EVENTS
· Guided tours at regular intervals.
· Saturday garden lecture tour series, April, May, and June. Admission fee.
· Twilight lecture tours, 8 Thursdays in May and June. Admission fee.
· Perennial plant sales, last weekend in April, last Saturday in May.
· Sunday afternoon concerts, last Sunday in April, June, August, and October.
· Long Island Rhododendron Festival, Wednesday through Sunday, mid-May.
· Picnic pops concerts, 8 Wednesday evenings in July and August. Admission fee.
· Antique auto show, June.
· Art in the Garden (photography, painting), courses spring and fall. Admission fee.
· Auto shows: Porsche, May; Corvette, August; Restoration Meet, September.
· Scottish Games, fourth Saturday in August.
· Luncheon lecture series, May through October. Admission fee.

- Horses in Action (an exhibition), Saturday of Columbus Day weekend. Admission fee.
- Floral design workshops, Saturdays throughout the year. Admission fee.
- Curatorial chats (slide lecture), 3 Sunday afternoons in November. Admission fee.
- Christmas at Westbury House, mid-December.

DIRECTIONS
Queens Midtown Tunnel to Long Island Expressway to Exit 39S (Glen Cove Road). Continue east on service road 1.2 miles. Take first right onto Old Westbury Road. Go ½ mile to entrance on left.

ॐ
PLANTING
FIELDS

O Y S T E R   B A Y ,   N E W   Y O R K

ॐ At Planting Fields, a 65-room Tudor-style mansion is surrounded by lawns. In the 1920s, it took an army of 20 men to mow
them, moving side by side. Today the lawns are reduced to 40 acres,
studded with giant specimen oaks, maples, beeches, red cedars, and
pines.

Many gardens spread randomly about the grounds. In the main,
they are pleasing, but none will win a *cum laude* award for design or
display. There is a pocket-sized herb garden, a formal pool garden, a
garden of dwarf conifers, synoptic and heather gardens, an azalea and
wildflower walk, two rhododendron parks, and year-round displays in
the greenhouses. A converted hay barn houses a library, classrooms,
and herbarium (pressed plant specimens).

Yes, there is something for everyone at this 409-acre Gold Coast
estate, which has had three sets of owners over the past 30 years: its
millionaire builder, William R. Coe; SUNY (the State University of
New York, both Farmingdale and Westbury campuses); and the Long
Island State Parks and Recreation Commission.

Because of the changing priorities of these three different owners
and a lack of consistent vision of how the house and gardens should be
used, daily maintenance and capital improvements at Planting Fields
had long suffered.

49

But at last, direction has stabilized under the Parks and Recreation Commission. Backed by Friends of Planting Fields, a strong community group that contributes about $50,000 annually for special renovation projects, the house and gardens are emerging as a felicitous combination of pleasure and teaching gardens, horticultural and cultural programs.

William Coe, the rags-to-riches émigré from England, built his estate to look as if it had taken three centuries to complete instead of three years (1918–1921). He borrowed a little of this, and a little of that, incorporating into the mansion reproduction gargoyles, gables, and facades imitative of English castles and cottages. To rival the landscaped grounds of his millionaire neighbors, Coe hired the Olmsted brothers of Boston to lay out his specimen trees, a heather garden, and cherry trees imported from Yokohama.

The Coes owned five family residences, but always chose to return to Long Island in the spring, and for good reason. It is the most dramatic season at Planting Fields. Cherry blossoms, wisteria, azaleas, dogwoods, and rhododendrons blaze across the landscape. Daffodils flood the woods with rivers of yellow.

By June the rose arbors are blooming with pink, yellow, and peach climbers. They arch over lilac and peony bushes that border the gravel path. Underneath the arbors, the smells are as intoxicating as a Victorian potpourri.

Then there are the teaching gardens, installed when the SUNY horticulture department was in residence: dwarf conifers that demonstrate to Long Island homeowners what can be achieved with evergreens in small spaces, an ornamental shrub garden, a synoptic garden (plants arranged alphabetically by botanical name), a nature trail, and wildflower walk.

The formal garden is vaguely Italianate and suffers the most from want of maintenance and imagination. Its centerpiece is a blue-tiled pool, only partially filled for safety reasons. Flower beds are planted with salvia, ageratum, ornamental grasses, begonias, and rockspray, with little regard for scale, mass, or texture. At one end of the pool, a tiny red-brick Hansel and Gretel teahouse is flanked by grape arbors.

In fall maples, oaks, and beeches slash their spectacular colors against the green lawns. Winter is also an alluring time to visit Planting Fields. When the rest of the world is wrapped in liverwurst gray, the greenhouses are flushed with tropical smells, warmth, and color.

By February the Camellia House is transformed with blossoms from 300 camellia trees, a remarkable variety ranging from old-fashioned ones to variegated mutations, some with two kinds of blossoms on the same tree. The newest crinkly, many-layered hybrids have a stellar array of colors—salmon, pink, and scarlet, to ivory and a creamy white delicately veined with mauve. This is the oldest and largest collection of camellias under glass in the United States.

Coe bought the entire camellia collection from the famous Waterer Nursery on the Isle of Guernsey in 1916. Great was his shock when he learned that these sensuous, glossy plants could not survive a Long Island winter. So a greenhouse was hastily built.

The young camellia trees that Coe imported included cultivars that had been propagated in Spain, England, and France for 200 years, when sea captains first brought them home from China and Japan. Among Coe's purchases was a singular beauty, *Camellia reticulata*, a double-ruffled salmon camellia that is still unrivaled for color and voluptuousness.

Throughout winter in the main greenhouse, there are seasonal floral shows and permanent plant displays, among them small noteworthy collections of ferns and begonias.

The Fernery exhibits 90 species of this most ancient and primitive plant, which bears neither seed, nor fruit, nor flower. Instead, ferns propagate by protoplasm stored in spores—tiny dots found on the underside of a fern.

Whoever would have thought that begonias, that ubiquitous staple in every Victorian home conservatory and public town square, could come in such a staggering array of textures and colors? The leaves can be spotted, striped, polka-dotted, or spatter-printed; puckered, flat, or three dimensional like trapunto. There are 85 species in this collection of 300 plants.

PLANTING FIELDS ARBORETUM, PO Box 58, Planting Fields Road, Oyster Bay, NY 11771. (516) 922-9200. Operated by New York State Office of Parks, Recreation, and Historical Preservation and the Long Island State Parks and Recreation Commission.

OPEN
May through Labor Day; on all weekends and holidays. Admission fee includes all facilities.
· Grounds, daily, 9 A.M. to 5 P.M.
· Camellia House, daily, 10 A.M. to 4 P.M.
· Main greenhouse, daily, 10 A.M. to 4:30 P.M.
· Planting Fields Horticultural Library, Wednesday, 10 A.M. to 4 P.M.; Saturday, 10 A.M. to 3 P.M.
· Coe Hall, guided tours, April through September, Saturday, 11 A.M.

to 2 P.M.; Monday through Friday, 1 A.M. to 3:30 P.M. Additional admission fee.

FACILITIES
· Gift shop.
· Hay Barn available for community events.
· Limited accessibility of grounds to people with physical disabilities; paved and gravel paths; the ground floor of Coe Hall is accessible to wheelchairs.

EVENTS
· Lectures, courses, workshops in horticulture, crafts, and cooking, nature walks, throughout the year.
· Fall flower and landscape show, second week in October.
· Winter Festival and Crafts Fair, first weekend in December.
· Beethoven Festival, last weekend in August.
· Sagamore Players Dinner Theater, weekend evenings, October, November, April.
· Chamber music concerts, some Sunday afternoons in Coe Hall.
· Guided tours of grounds and mansion, for groups year-round, advance reservations necessary.

DIRECTIONS
Queens Midtown Tunnel to Long Island Expressway to Exit 18 (Glen Cove Road) north. Stay on Glen Cove Road to Route 25A (Northern Boulevard). Turn right (east) onto Route 25A, past C. W. Post College to Route 107. Turn left (north) onto Chicken Valley Road. Then make right turn onto Planting Fields Road. Entrance is about 1 mile on the right.

SUNY
(STATE UNIVERSITY
OF NEW YORK)

FARMINGDALE, NEW YORK

What a surprise to find so fetching a series of small gardens tucked into an obscure corner of this SUNY campus, formerly a state school of agriculture.

The gardens are the teaching gardens of the Department of Ornamental Horticulture, a two-year program (in the process of expanding to four years) with 100 students. The expansion reflects the rise of Long Island's floriculture industry, which has now replaced the Long Island potato as Suffolk County's number one agricultural crop.

Here are 13 acres of modest pleasure, sandwiched between the greenhouses and ornamental horticultural building. In a small formal garden roses are planted in engaging combinations of ornamental kale and cabbages. On a hillock of crushed red stone, a bed of dusty rose and pearly green sedum is crowned with gloriosa daisies. In a pine orchard each tree is planted well apart from its neighbor to reveal contour, texture, and limb structure. The 50 species have been chosen because they are slow-growing, look graceful in small areas, or, like the limber and umbrella pines, have bark or needles of rich texture or odors.

But the *pièce de résistance* is the evergreen shrub, heather, and dwarf conifer garden, a grassy enclosure walled with Canadian hemlock on one side and white pine on the other. An ornamental shrub bed, 65-by-30 feet, runs in a gentle S-shaped berm down the middle. Its vitality derives from its changing elevation (one to three feet), and its wide range of textures and monochromatic greens. Textures range from the crisp angles of holly leaves to the softer, blue, shagged juniper to the delicate fringes of a threadleaf maple. In one corner of the garden a standard hardy orange stands in lethal splendor. Sporting four-inch thorns, and yellow globes that smell so good and taste so sour. The colors in the garden range from sea-foam, lemon, and dusty greens; to the mauve, ocher, and olive shades of heather.

The Department gardens combine three landscape essentials required by Long Island's corporate and industrial park clients: high show, low maintenance, and hardiness of plants that can thrive in Long Island's sandy, acid soil. The skill with which these requirements have been met make the two-mile trip from the Long Island Expressway worth it.

THE STATE UNIVERSITY OF NEW YORK COLLEGE OF TECH-NOLOGY AT FARMINGDALE, Melville Road, Farmingdale, NY 11735. (516) 420-2000.

OPEN
- Gardens, daily, 8 A.M. to dusk. No admission fee.
- Greenhouses, Monday through Friday, 8 A.M. to 4:30 P.M. No admission fee.

FACILITIES
- Campus snack bar.
- Limited access for people with physical disabilities (grass paths in gardens).

EVENTS
- Occasional workshops, seminars for professionals and nonprofessionals on horticultural subjects. Admission fee.
- Associate degree programs, day and evening programs, year-round, in horticulture. Admission fee.

DIRECTIONS
Queens Midtown Tunnel to Long Island Expressway to Exit 49, turning south on Route 110. Travel south about 2 miles to Melville Road. Turn right onto Melville at the entrance to the college.

ჼ

CARAMOOR

KATONAH, NEW YORK

⁓ Although Caramoor is best known for the musical events held in its Spanish Courtyard and Venetian Theater, some of the best "events"—dramatic plantings and romantic structures—are scattered over the grounds: a large dovecote without doves, a tennis pavilion without a tennis court, two eighteenth-century gazebos, a cedar walk, a walled garden, four gigantic verdigris pineapples that turn out to be streetlights, and a wall of carved evergreens.

The evergreen wall is sublime—densely massed conifers trimmed so that each rounded shape stands out from its neighbor, forming billows of green, blue-green, and yellow-green. The wall curves around part of a cement dance floor. Now the only guests are two white stone statues, a maid and a gallant, sharply silhouetted against the green backdrop.

This captivating array of landscape adventures occurs without any overall plan. No records have been found of the garden's creation, and no archives exist.

In the 1930s and 1940s, Caramoor was the country estate of two ardent collectors, banker-lawyer Walter Tower Rosen and his wife, Lucie. Paintings, rugs, textiles, sculpture, and entire rooms from French and Italian palaces came home to Caramoor. Sculpture and architectural objects spilled over into the garden.

The Rosens were both musicians and loved entertaining actors, artists, and other musicians at Caramoor. Concerts were given in the great Music Room. Guests strolled the 100 acres of gardens and woods.

The wide cedar walk is a fitting approach to the drama of the walled garden. Beginning at a marble gazebo, the walk is a grand passage of filigreed light, soft underfoot with bark and pine needles. It runs the length of a city block, ending at a stone Veronese archway, the entrance to the walled garden.

A curious man-made mount dominates the garden. In the Middle Ages, mounts provided feudal lords with a view over the wall: Was the orchard being properly tended? Was the enemy approaching? Mounts were also garbage dumps, a medieval version of a modern landfill.

Today, the mount is covered with ferns and cedars. From a stone bench on the top, you can survey the crumbling walls of a garden-within-a-garden—the sunken garden. Flowers are clearly low priority at Caramoor. The few there are—roses, perennials, and annuals—fill the beds of the sunken garden.

Massive gates lead to the open-air Venetian Theater where concertgoers sit between walls of trees. The gates are a disconcerting combination of scale and era—monumental American winged horses' heads, solid and modern, joined with intricately patterned eighteenth-century arabesques of wrought iron and gilt.

CARAMOOR, Girdle Ridge Road, PO Box R, Katonah, NY 10536. (914) 232-3888.

OPEN
House museum and grounds, May through November, Thursday and Saturday, 11 A.M. to 4 P.M.; Sunday, 1 P.M. to 4 P.M.; last entry to house at 3 P.M. all days; Wednesday and Friday, by appointment. Groups year-round, by appointment. Admission fee.

❧

PRECEDING PAGE: *The Cedar Walk and Veronese archway leading to the walled garden.*

FACILITIES
- Picnicking permitted only for visitors to house and concertgoers.
- Museum shop.
- House partially accessible to people with physical disabilities; other than main road, garden paths are not paved.

EVENTS
- Caramoor Music Festival, concerts held Thursday through Sunday in July, Friday through Sunday in August; Saturday concerts held in Venetian Theater, others in Spanish Courtyard of the house.
- Spring and fall, concerts and lectures on art and music in the Music Room.
- High School Celebration of Music and Art, end of May.
- Crafts Fair, September weekend.
- Antiques Fair, September weekend.
- Holiday Open House, early December; guided tours, strolling musicians, refreshments, Christmas decorations, shop open.

DIRECTIONS
Triborough Bridge to Bruckner Expressway (I-278) to Hutchinson River Parkway north to I-684. Take Exit 6 (Katonah/Cross River); turn right onto Route 35. Go to first traffic light, and turn right onto Route 22 south. Go about 2 miles to cement island with Caramoor sign; make a slight left onto Girdle Ridge Road. Caramoor is ½ mile ahead on the right.

THE DONALD M. KENDALL SCULPTURE GARDENS AT PEPSICO

PURCHASE, NEW YORK

At noon, employees stroll along the Golden Path that rims a vast lawn, dawdle by a pond feeding ducks, or picnic near a giant orange stabile by Alexander Calder.

At sunset, dog-walkers and runners jog on circumference roads, past the lengthening shadows of a 45-ton Roman travertine sculpture, Richard Erdman's *Passage*.

This is the Donald M. Kendall Sculpture Gardens of PepsiCo's world headquarters, 140 acres of lawn and woods studded with 40 pieces of twentieth-century sculpture. The list of artists reads like a Who's

Who of sculpture, including Jacques Lipchitz, Max Ernst, Henry Moore, and Alberto Giacometti.

The lawns, the low-slung modern concrete and glass office building, vistas, and sculptures are held in delicate balance by two elements: a highly sensitive placement of trees and shrubs and a Golden Path that cuts a ribbon of beige gravel around the perimeter of green turf. The path links sculpture, pond, woods, and lawn.

Both the plantings and path are the contributions of the late British-born Russell Page, world-renowned garden designer who came to PepsiCo in 1980 to reshape the landscape as a setting for the growing sculpture collection.

Sometimes Page massed trees as a backdrop for the sculpture. Sometimes he planted them singly to complement a piece. At other times, the trees became sculptures themselves, silhouetted against grass as silky as a putting green.

For example, the dusky blue of Colorado blue spruce provides a bracing contrast to *Hats Off*, Calder's 25-foot-high bright orange stabile. The trees, now grown to 25 feet, form a solid blue-green arc behind the sculpture. By maturity, the trees will reach 50 feet. A scattering of white pines mingles with David Wynne's *Dancer with a Bird*. This delicate bronze nude has oxidized to the same greenish black color as the pine needles. The two—pines and statue—are paired in monochromatic tandem.

A family of floppy gray-green weeping hemlocks crouch in a semicircle around Isamu Noguchi's *Energy Void*, a 14-foot-high triangular-shaped doughnut of dark chocolate brown granite. The free-form shape and shaggy needles of the hemlocks provide a rich textural contrast with the smooth, sleek elegance of the sculpture.

Near the main auto entrance, tall, yellow-green Hinoki cypresses dance in the wind, their top branches catching the most vigorous breezes. In front of them, tuffets of low, wiry golden thread junipers dance a slower raggedy shuffle.

Clusters of willows border the pond. Graceful and languid, the long strands of willow leaves move in unison with the water spray windblown off a single 40-foot geyser that spouts from the middle of the pond. The synchronized movement of the two is hypnotic.

As you approach the office buildings, plantings become smaller in scale, more geometric, crisp, and businesslike. In an outdoor dining

❧

PRECEDING PAGE: *Heavily needled hemlocks provide shaggy contrast to Isamu Noguchi's granite sculpture,* Energy Void.

pavilion, the tops of plane trees have been sheared flat. In the courtyards, trees poke through waist-high squares of densely packed yew, a-square-within-a-square courtyards.

In the only formal flower garden at PepsiCo, three small pools are embellished with irises or yellow, blue, purple, and cherry-colored water lilies. A green metallic frog nestles in the corner of one of the pools, which are bordered by an embankment of blue, lavender, white, and purple of hibiscus, columbine, Russian sage, aster, sedum, plumbago, achillea, buddleia, and shrub roses. The embankment and masses of orange and yellow daylilies bedded under a short allée of Japanese cherries provide summer-long ribbons of color in this otherwise subdued environment of green. From their offices, employees can gaze across the lily pools to a fanciful nineteenth-century-style gazebo, painted a soft pinkish beige.

The PepsiCo sculpture gardens had their aegis in another vast enterprise, the 1965 merger of Frito-Lay with the Pepsi-Cola Company, engineered by Donald M. Kendall, then chairman and chief executive officer of Pepsi-Cola. The year of the merger, Kendall set about in true beaux arts tradition to combine architecture, landscape, and sculpture on a scale that would properly reflect the stature of the new corporation.

He chose Edward Durell Stone, Sr., as architect and his son, Edward Durell Stone, Jr., as landscape designer for the 140 acres that once comprised the playing fields of the Blind Brook Polo Club. At a public hearing, Kendall reassured uneasy Purchase residents that he would "turn that cow pasture into a new Versailles." He then began to select and commission the pieces of sculpture for the garden.

Kendall chose sculpture as the medium that best reflected his vision of a good corporation: stable but willing to explore and take risks. At that time, sculptors were experimenting with new technologies and combinations of materials—alloys, plastics, and synthetics—and producing the kind of avant-garde work that Kendall admired.

By 1970 the offices were finished, seven interconnected concrete and glass blocks built around three courtyards. The entire complex was sited slightly off-center in a grassy plain overlooking a man-made pond. Employee parking lots were concealed behind banks of hemlock, rhododendron, and grasses.

In 1980 when Kendall hired Page to reshape the landscape, his choice was inspired. For 60 years, Page had designed gardens on five continents for the rich, the royal, and the famous. His knowledge of plant material was prodigious; he preferred simplicity to the elaborate, local plants over imported exotics; and for each project he relentlessly pursued a single design idea.

In the case of PepsiCo, sculptures were the one design idea he pursued. How and where to position them on this vast, saucer-shaped lawn? How and where to arrange plantings to accentuate or highlight a piece? How to unify the whole?

In his first year at Purchase, Page scooted about in his golf cart, strolled under his large English umbrella in rain and snow, sketched, and pored over plant lists. With near life-size models of some of the sculptures, he considered light and shadow, solid and void, harmony and contrast, and the look of a plant in four seasons. He pondered the speed of the viewer traveling on foot or by car.

Page first laid out the Golden Path. Then he opened up vistas into fringe woods, added lily ponds, and planted shrubs and ground covers in sweeping movements of color that formed bridges between the manicured lawns and bordering woods. Above all, Page planted trees, the real grandeur of his work at PepsiCo, knowing that he would never live to see them to full maturity.

Page returned to England in December of 1985 and died shortly thereafter. On a piece of paper found in his desk at PepsiCo, he had written, "I am tired, it is raining, and I am not a water lily." This quote, on a brass plaque, is imbedded in cement near the gazebo and water lily ponds.

THE DONALD M. KENDALL SCULPTURE GARDENS AT PEPSICO, 700 Anderson Hill Road, Purchase, NY 10577. (914) 253-3000.

OPEN
Daily, 9 A.M. to 5 P.M.

FACILITIES
· Picnicking permitted.
· Most of the garden is accessible to people with physical disabilities; gravel and macadam paths.

DIRECTIONS
Triborough Bridge to Bruckner Expressway (I-278) to Hutchinson River Parkway north to Exit 28 (Lincoln Avenue), marked also with SUNY/Purchase sign. After exit ramp, turn left onto Lincoln Avenue and go to the end of the road. Turn right onto Anderson Hill Road. PepsiCo entrance is on the right. Follow signs to the sculpture garden parking lot.

꒰

THE
HAMMOND MUSEUM
ORIENTAL
STROLL GARDEN

NORTH SALEM, NEW YORK

꒰ Natalie Hays Hammond's idea when she started building her Museum and Oriental Stroll Garden on a Westchester hilltop in 1960 was to achieve tranquillity, "a world apart, as well as a world within." She succeeded. So well, in fact, that despite signs of decay, the garden still offers that tranquillity.

For the most part, the original garden structure remains. Stepping stones and paths wind from one landscape to another, a new view revealed at each turn—patterned tree trunks, reflecting pool, a lake, and an island. Broad stone steps lead across a stone outcropping to a Shozo-Seki, the stone that marks the perfect point from which to view the garden. Vertical stones in one part of the garden represent the 16 disciples of Buddha. In another part, a tiny rectangle of raked white gravel harbors the symbolic contemplation stones of a Zen garden.

Sitting on a bench in the sun, listening to insects drone, life seems peaceful indeed.

But empty water-lily boxes lie at the bottom of a reflecting pool. Stone sculptures sit in weeds. No new plantings soften the reproach of raw, sawed-off tree stumps.

The deterioration began in 1983 when Miss Hammond became ill and would allow no one to touch the garden. Until her death in 1985, the garden lay fallow. Catching up is difficult. Miss Hammond's inheritance from her father, who in 1889 discovered King Solomon's Mines in Rhodesia, was spent on the museum and garden, and no money was left for maintenance. Funds come in "bits and pieces," says Elizabeth Taylor, a cousin of Miss Hammond and the current director. "What we're looking for is a Japanese corporation in Westchester to underwrite us." It should be so.

THE HAMMOND MUSEUM ORIENTAL STROLL GARDEN, Deveau Road, North Salem, NY 10560. (914) 669-5033.

OPEN
Late May through late October, Wednesday through Sunday, 11 A.M. to 5 P.M. Admission fee.

FACILITIES
· Luncheon is served on the flagstone terrace, Wednesday through Saturday, brunch on Sunday; reservations required.
· Limited access for people with physical disabilities; steps.

EVENTS
· Changing art exhibitions.
· Annual interfaith blessing of the land and animals, first or second Sunday in May; children and adults bring pets, from crickets to cows; clerical parade led by bagpipes. No admission fee.

DIRECTIONS
Triborough Bridge to Bruckner Expressway (I-278) to Hutchinson River Parkway north to I-684 to Exit 7. Go east on Route 116 about 5 miles to first intersection. Turn left onto Route 124. Go ¼ mile to Deveau Road on the right; turn right onto Deveau and go to top of hill into the Hammond parking lot.

INNISFREE

MILLBROOK, NEW YORK

The drive into Innisfree bumps over a dirt road for two miles when suddenly the woodland opens to a cup-shaped clearing. Through the clearing, granite cliffs drop into a black, glassy lake in the distance. Pink and white marshmallows and Japanese primroses sparkle in a boggy meadow.

No fences, no warning signs, no security guards mar the sense of exploration. Innisfree beckons.

No sooner have you dropped your picnic hamper and set out around the lake than Innisfree begins to reveal itself as much more than a happy coincidence of hill, sky, and water. Step by step, rock by rock, plant by plant, somebody has thought of everything.

Wooden slat chairs are placed so that a view is framed just where sight lines of cliff, tree, and a curve of water lilies intersect. Along a path, a series of "events" reveal themselves—a clump of irises, a waterfall or statue—each set apart in its own environment.

In a rocky niche, a Buddha ponders the world from behind a delicate screen of wisteria. Water trickles over a mossy rock, falling silver drop by silver drop into a six-inch granite saucer below. Slender spear-shaped sentry maples flex in the wind. Strands of Virginia creeper—glossy green in summer, burgundy in autumn—dangle over a small rocky grotto. The creeper just brushes the tops of lacy emerald-stemmed fern that grows at the entrance.

Like anything great, Innisfree seems effortless, as if it just happened—sky, rocks, plants, robust and taut in perfect balance. Is this some kind of Eden, man-made, right here in Millbrook?

Man-made it is: the ancient Chinese art of landscaping called "cup" gardening, a way of moving *into* a landscape, rather than looking *at* it. In Western garden traditions, such as the English great park or Le Notre's grand formal vistas, a panorama is revealed in one sweep of the eye. In cup gardening, the landscape unfolds, vista by vista, secret by secret. The cup can be the size of a barrel or an entire lake. The cups are linked to each other in a progression along a path. A kind of rhythm sets in: expectation, revelation, connecting link.

Cup gardening at Innisfree has been translated by two men, close friends and colleagues, each a genius in his own way: Walter Beck, painter, sculptor, and original creator of Innisfree; and Lester Collins, former chairman of Harvard's Department of Landscape Architecture, now trustee-in-residence at Innisfree.

Walter Beck was born in Dayton, Ohio, in 1864, the child of German immigrants. In this narrow, rural environment, Beck decided to become an artist. He traveled to Europe, studied at the Royal Academy of Fine Arts in Munich, and finally returned to the United States, where he taught painting and illustration at Pratt Institute in Brooklyn. At the age of 58 he married Marion Burt Stone, heiress to the Mesabi Iron Range fortune. It was a second marriage for both. They went to live on her thousand-acre estate at Millbrook.

Highly influenced by Chinese scrolls they discovered in London museums and libraries, the Becks decided to reshape Innisfree. It became a lifework for them both. They graded terraces and dug out granite boulders from their glacial resting places, cradling them in quilts so as not to disturb the centuries-old lichen. They meticulously

❧

PRECEDING PAGE: *A grass allée shaded by shadblow trees rims the shoreline.*

65

repositioned these treasures to form man-made cups and arches and nooks; used them as pieces of sculpture and to divert streams.

Marion, a botanist, added plantings to achieve what Beck called an "occult balance," a quality he found in calligraphy and in the stone rubbings of the gardens of Wang Wei, an eighth-century Chinese poet, painter, and garden maker. As a painter would do, Beck arranged a series of objects within a garden cup—a rock, grasses, a bench, a pruned tree. When viewed from any angle, these objects were in asymmetrical balance. The Eastern "shape sense" Beck, in time, was to call it, as opposed to Western "form sense," which depended upon measurement, perspective, and anatomy.

In some cups, mosses, ferns, and wildflowers became a tapestry; in others, it was water—water dripping, water splashing, water rushing, or lying still in pools.

It was during these formative years that Lester Collins, a graduate student at Harvard, began to make weekend visits to Innisfree. He and the Becks often sat at a picnic table arranging objects—a pipe, a tumbler, an apple—in an imaginary cube of space, trying to achieve "hidden balance."

After Beck's death in 1954, Lester Collins began to develop the pine forest that you now see across the lake from Beck's cup gardens.

He laid out a path on the grassy lakeshore and pruned the forest bordering granite cliffs. At the end of the lake, he placed a Japanese corn crib, a small slatted shed, now weathered gray. Inside, benches offer respite from sun and vista.

The path from the crib climbs a gentle knoll of white pines. Stripped of their boughs to a 30-foot height, the black trunks of the pines are an electric contrast to the ground cover of bright yellow-green Canadian mayflowers. It is a contrast not found in nature. Since mayflowers require filtered sunlight, the shade of an unpruned forest would be too dense for them to thrive.

At the top of a knoll, a single jet of water shoots 30 feet into the air. The water just reaches the lower fringes of pine boughs before falling back with heavy splattering sounds into a huge, black flagstone saucer.

A freestanding gateway entwined with wisteria closes nothing in and nothing out. It frames a path as it meanders from the woods to a footbridge. At the footbridge, another vista unfolds. A distant lake, unreachable, recedes into a backdrop of hills.

Yes, Innisfree is a kind of Eden. You can absorb Innisfree. You can perceive Innisfree. But you do not "do" Innisfree as you "do" Longwood Gardens.

By the time he was 90, Beck was convinced that garden creation was an art ranking alongside painting and music. He also believed that American landscape design had not yet come of age. Innisfree, he hoped, would be a design laboratory of ideas to stimulate a truly indigenous American garden idiom. His laboratory is there for all takers, left in trust by his widow.

INNISFREE GARDEN, Tyrrel Road, Millbrook, NY 12545. (914) 677-8000.

OPEN
May through October, Saturday and Sunday (and Monday if it is a legal holiday), 11 A.M. to 5 P.M.; Wednesday through Friday, 10 A.M. to 4 P.M. Admission fee.

FACILITIES
· Picnicking permitted.
· Except for the overall view from the parking area, not accessible to people with physical disabilities.

EVENTS
Informal discussions about Beck's work are held occasionally with design professionals.

DIRECTIONS
Henry Hudson Parkway to Saw Mill River Parkway to Taconic State Parkway to Poughkeepsie/Millbrook exit at Route 44 east. Turn right, and go 1¾ miles; turn right onto Tyrrel Road and go 1 mile to entrance gate house.

MARY FLAGLER
CARY ARBORETUM

MILLBROOK, NEW YORK

For years the Cary Arboretum was a little-known, up-country cousin of the New York Botanical Garden—1,900 acres of meadow, forest, swamp, glacial outcroppings, hilly uplands, and a trout stream. Collections of native and imported willows, birch, pines, and spruce were its chief assets.

Then in 1983, the New York Botanical Garden made a dramatic shift in priorities. It established the Institute of Ecosystem Studies at the arboretum with the mandate to investigate ecosystems of the north-eastern United States; and to disseminate information useful in shaping governmental policy on environmental issues.

Fortunately for the layman, the institute has broadly interpreted this educational mandate. It has developed four miles of trails through woodlands and meadows, permanent displays of exotic and native plants, and rotating exhibitions on the institute's ecological research projects. Two current studies are on the life cycle of ticks that cause Lyme disease and the effect of pollution on aquatic systems.

But best of all for garden lovers is the new Perennial Garden, dedicated in 1987. The garden focuses on ecologically sound gardening practices and vivid combinations of low-maintenance plants that insure a showy garden three seasons a year.

Laid out by two horticulturists from the arboretum and the New York Botanical Garden, the Perennial Garden very much shows its instructional function. Superimposed on the bones of a 1929 predecessor, the garden is strong in plant material and weak in basic design. Brick paths angle around odd-shaped flower beds in slightly skewed geometric forms. A pergola, a gazebo, and a sunken octagonal flower bed visually pull at cross-purposes as centers of interest.

But the design deficiencies of this jigsaw garden flutter into oblivion as one contemplates the diversity of perennials—4,500 varieties— making this the largest collection of perennials in a public garden in the Northeast. Eight hundred species have been mixed and matched in inventive combinations of color, texture, and shape. Some plants have been isolated or planted against contrasting backgrounds to emphasize their architectural structure. Others are simply massed for impact.

At the entrance to the visitor center, a farmhouse built in 1817, hosta are massed in an elbow of the building. There are 20 varieties—a rich tactile patchwork of lemon-colored, olive, and apple green leaves. Some leaves are smooth as satin; others, ridged like corduroy or puckered like seersucker.

A peony bed—a diamond-shaped sweep of color—runs about 200 feet in length and is packed with huge satin-headed blooms of ivory, cerise, pink, garnet, and purple. What a splendid homage to the peony, known to thrive for years in poor soil, impervious to slugs, mildew, and rabbits.

Behind the visitor center, beds are solid with lilies or ornamental grasses. One bed is planted with *Inula magnifica*, coneflowers, and black-eyed Susans, those hardy wildings that jumped the garden fence 200 years ago to become cheery mainstays in America's backyards. At Cary, some coneflowers measure eight feet tall and range in color from pearly white and yellow to garnet.

∾

PRECEDING PAGE: *The zigzag floral beds of the restored 1920s Perennial Garden, photographed from the roof of Gifford House.*

Have you ever seen parsley two feet tall? You can see it in the herb garden.

Nearby yew and maidenhair fern are combined to make a hedge of high contrast. A row of tall feathery yellow-green ferns nods over the dense, boxy yew, kept cropped to a height of two feet.

In the Shankman Memorial Garden, pink and red roses are planted in thick mats of purple and white alyssum that crowd out weeds. The white alyssum looks fine, but as a ground cover the purple alyssum drains the color right out of the pink roses. Yes, there is something to be learned in every corner of the Cary Arboretum.

Beyond the garden, four miles of labeled trails wind through a meadow, a fern glen, the Cary Pines, and along Wappinger Creek.

Buttered with wildflowers, the Meadow Garden is an old-fashioned walk that meanders past the stone foundations of a mill, a doddering apple orchard, and locust saplings, aggressively reclaiming open space. All the childhood field favorites are here—honeysuckle, Queen-Anne's-lace, fleabane, goldenrod, chickory—charmingly labeled.

For example, you will learn that the fruit of the barberry, that thorny invader from the Orient, makes excellent, though tart, jam; that there are 20,000 varieties of asters ranging in color from ivory to royal purple; that black locusts were brought by immigrants from Scotland to provide a source for fence posts. Black locust grows fast and, when sunk in the ground as a post, takes half a century to rot.

Where the Meadow Garden links to the Wappinger Creek Trail, a different ecological world unfolds. A dense canopy of black birch, oaks, and hemlock binds the piney smells to the sound of a fast-running brook. A pale light sifts over moss, toadstools, and lichen-covered rocks, turning them into the softest shades of gray, green, and champagne. Orange buttons of fungus dot a black log. Occasionally a great blue heron sweeps across a bar of sunlight.

The Creek Trail eventually connects to the Cary Pines Trail, which passes through a hemlock grove, thickets, and open fields before emerging under a row of Scotch pines, a ragged version of an allée.

The Fern Glen is a mossy, water-soaked glade banked with native ferns and species imported from such high-altitude climates as the Alps, Himalayas, and the USSR. Duff paths, springy underfoot, lead to an overlook where Wappinger Creek plunges under a stone bridge.

For this remarkable horticultural resource, we have Mary Flagler Cary to thank. She inherited a fortune from her father, Henry M. Flagler, a nineteenth-century Florida real estate tycoon, who built palatial hotels and financed the Florida East Coast Railway.

Mary spent her childhood summers at Millbrook, later returning with her husband, Melbert Cary, to acquire, bit by bit, the 1,900 acres that became their estate.

Like many other rich landowners who had no children but wanted to keep their land intact, Mary Flagler Cary created a public land trust. After her death in 1967, the land trust developed an arboretum, which was given to the New York Botanical Garden in 1971. Today the trust, along with the Mary Flagler Cary Foundation, defrays 53 percent of the institute's annual budget of around $3.5 million.

MARY FLAGLER CARY ARBORETUM/INSTITUTE OF ECOSYSTEM STUDIES/NEW YORK BOTANICAL GARDEN, Box AB, Millbrook, NY 12545. (914) 677-5358.

OPEN
- Grounds and greenhouses, daily, May through September, Monday through Saturday, 9 A.M. to 6 P.M.; greenhouse, 9 A.M. to 4 P.M.; Sunday, 1 P.M. to 6 P.M. (Greenhouse closes at 4 P.M.)
- Grounds and greenhouse, October through April, Monday through Saturday, 9 A.M. to 4 P.M.; Sunday, 1 P.M. to 4 P.M. Closed holidays. Trails and internal roads closed during deer hunting season and extreme weather conditions. No admission fee but access permit required. Permit available at Gifford House Visitor and Education Center until one hour before closing time, year-round.
- Gift shop, May through September, Tuesday through Saturday, 9 A.M. to 5 P.M.; Sunday, 1 P.M. to 5 P.M.; October through April, Tuesday through Saturday, 9 A.M. to 4 P.M.; Sunday, 1 P.M. to 4 P.M.

FACILITIES
- Picnicking permitted behind Gifford House.
- Gift and plant shop.
- Bicycling, jogging on paved internal roads with access pass.
- Perennial Garden, Gifford House, greenhouse, and internal roads accessible to wheelchairs.

EVENTS
- Fall, winter, and spring courses in landscape design, gardening, ecology, botany. Admission fee.
- Occasional art exhibitions in Plant Science Building. No admission fee.
- Seasonal research displays at Gifford House. No admission fee.

- Ecology walks/talks, first and third Sunday of each month, 2 P.M. to 4 P.M. No admission fee.
- Ecology seminars, every Friday, 3:30 P.M. to 4:30 P.M., except in summer. No admission fee.

DIRECTIONS

Henry Hudson Parkway to Saw Mill River Parkway to Taconic State Parkway to Poughkeepsie/Millbrook exit at Route 44 east. Go about 2 miles. Turn left onto Route 44A and go about 1 mile to the Gifford House Visitor and Education Center, the red-brick building on the left.

MOHONK
MOUNTAIN HOUSE
GARDENS

NEW PALTZ, NEW YORK

To environmentalists, Mohonk Mountain House is more than a mountain resort; it is an ecological way of life. In the nineteenth century, long before conservation became fashionable, the Smiley brothers, good Quakers that they were, developed their 7,500-acre resort and farmlands based on sound conservation principles. They recycled everything. The manure on carriage roads was hauled off to the gardens. Table scraps went to the hog pens. When trees were cleared for carriage roads, the lumber from red oaks was made into furniture for the mountain house, and the ash was sold for baseball bats.

To the Smiley twins, Albert and Alfred, the investigation and contemplation of nature was one of the best ways of knowing God. On such Quaker precepts, they built their resort. Walks, mountain climbs, hearty food, family sings, and prayer took the place of cards, dancing, and liquor.

For over a century, social-minded politicians, authors, and millionaires have gathered at this great turreted stone dinosaur to consider how they might improve the world. John Burroughs, Theodore Roosevelt, William Jennings Bryan, John D. Rockefeller, Jr., Andrew Carnegie, Isaac Asimov—all slept, and contemplated, here.

Like the Mountain House, the large, old-fashioned gardens are Victorian in origin. In 1907 Albert Smiley wrote, "I have treated this property, the result of 76 purchases, as a landscape artist does his canvas, only my canvas covers seven square miles."

On a sloping lawn near the hotel, on five acres of his canvas, he laid out flower beds, herb and rose gardens. The gardens are separated by trellises, arbors, gazebos (called "summerhouses" at Mohonk), and gravel paths. The paths that were wide enough for the hoopskirts of olden times are wide enough today for motorized garden equipment.

Against a backdrop of quartz cliffs, mountain laurel, and rhododendrons, the floral rectangles of delphiniums, snapdragons, peonies, and daylilies make brilliant swatches of color on the green turf. There are beds of flaming red and bottle blue salvia and phlox, marigolds, pansies, heliotropes, and impatiens called by the enchanting name of Busy Lizzies by our grandmothers.

In spring, honeysuckle, wisteria, mock orange, spirea, forsythia, beauty bush, and lilac shower the hillside with color and perfume.

The formal gardens combine three kinds of flower beds: rectangles filled with a single species of one color, or a single species in many colors; flat and berm beds in solid geometrics, called carpet bedding; and knot beds, where plants alternate with graveled spaces to form intricate patterns.

In all there are 77 flower beds, anchored in one corner by a two-story twig-and-limb gazebo straight out of Andrew Downing's 1879 landscape sketchbook. Arbors are smothered with roses. Some are single-petaled favorites, such as the lemon-colored 'Seven Sisters' or shell pink 'Sweetbriar', which produce a glossy green gall used in pomanders in Victorian times. A spunky little white shrub rose—the Scotch rose—blooms at the base of the arbors.

One bed is planted with "modern" old-fashioned hybrids, such as the 'Queen Elizabeth' and 'Saratoga' roses. 'Sunbright', a hardy yellow rose, blooms its head off all summer long. Nearby in the crescent-shaped Albert K. Smiley Memorial Rose Garden, the hybrid teas

⤝

PRECEDING PAGE: *Victorian carpet bedding and knot gardens originally planted by Albert Smiley in the 1870s.*

are protected from deer by an eight-foot twig-and-limb latticework fence.

Deer are a perennial scourge and devour roses just as happily as they devour mountain laurel. Head groundsman Chet Davis has found smell to be his best ally against deer, and he has tried everything.

Most effective is Big Game, a repellent made of putrified egg solids, which he scatters around the flower beds.

In the early years, deer were the least of Albert Smiley's problems. There was no soil to speak of. One guest, Frederick Partington, wrote in 1911, "At Mohonk, there seemed to be only two places for growing flowers—the quartz rocks and the branches of trees. A remote third might have been on the lake—a floating garden."

Begun in 1886, the garden came into being only after Albert Smiley imported tons of topsoil from the surrounding countryside. Frugal in all other things, he spent extravagantly on his garden. Expenditures allocated to the garden went unquestioned. He was fond of grumbling to guests that every geranium cost him $5.

In 1986, just 100 years after the garden was begun, Mohonk Mountain House, gardens, and environment were declared a National Historic Landmark. The designation would have pleased the old man enormously.

Adjacent to the formal garden is a wildflower and fern trail. The trail leads to the greenhouse, open for viewing and buying. Most plants are grown for display in the Mountain House, but there is a good choice of Victorian houseplants for sale: alternantheras, strawberry begonias; Christmas cactuses; cast-iron plants; bird's-nest ferns; and geraniums— mint, apricot, rose, and lemon (alas, the leaves smell only when rubbed, but dried they make excellent potpourri).

MOHONK MOUNTAIN HOUSE, Lake Mohonk, New Paltz, NY 12561. (914) 255-1000 or (212) 233-2244.

OPEN
· Gardens, daily, dawn to dusk. Entrance fee paid at gate.
· Greenhouse, Monday through Saturday, 9 A.M. to 3:30 P.M.; Sunday, 10 A.M. to 1 P.M.
· Mountain House, daily. Entrance permitted only with overnight or meal reservation, which must be made in advance.

FACILITIES
· Restaurant/snack bar at Mountain House (see above for admission policy).

- Soup/sandwiches at Picnic Lodge for day visitors, June through October, 10 A.M. to 5 P.M., and on winter weekends when snow conditions are good.
- Picnicking permitted near Picnic Lodge.
- Gift shop in Mountain House (see previous page for admission policy).

EVENTS

- Weekend seminars, September through June, on such subjects as cooking, stress management, chamber music, languages, sports, science fiction, mystery solving. Admission fee.
- Garden Holiday, last week in August. Admission fee. Priority for daily seminars and Garden Holiday is given to House guests, but it is possible to attend a one-day session with the purchase of a meal. Reservations must be made in advance.

DIRECTIONS

George Washington Bridge to Palisades Parkway. Exit at Route 9W, New York State Thruway. Continue on Thruway to Exit 18 (New Paltz). Turn left onto Route 199 and follow Main Street through New Paltz. After crossing the Wallkill River, take the first right. Bear left at the fork and follow Mohonk signs up Mountain Rest Road to Mohonk gates on the left.

MONTGOMERY PLACE

ANNANDALE-ON-HUDSON, NEW YORK

Montgomery Place is that rare thing in America, an ancestral estate that belonged to one family—the Livingstons—for almost two centuries. Like the houses of all the great Hudson River estates, the 23-room Classical Revival mansion sits high above the river. The mansion and its 434 acres of gardens, commercial orchards, historic forest, and spellbinding vistas reflect the privileged life of Hudson Valley aristocracy from the beginning of the nineteenth century to the present.

Along this stretch of the Hudson, the farthest point reached by the salt tides of the Atlantic Ocean, the land rises from the shore in a long, easy elevation. The view from the mansion, set far back from the river, extends across a grassy bowl to three graduated bodies of water—a small lily pond, a bay, and finally, the sparkling river.

The man-made pond connects the visual prologue to the expanse of river and the smoke blue Catskill ridges layered in the distance. The water is seen through a framework of red oaks, the view accentuated by the nineteenth-century device of "peekaboos," or windows, cut through the trees at midheight.

The landscape today is a mixture of nineteenth- and twentieth-century restorations: two woodland walks laid out by the second owner, Edward Livingston, in the 1830s, and the gardens created in the 1920s and 1930s by Violetta Delafield, wife of a Livingston descendant. The walks and gardens are separated not only by a century but by geography as well; they are in different quadrants of the property, unrelated to each other.

Edward Livingston, once mayor of New York City and later Secretary of State under Andrew Jackson, opened vistas to the river and cut and cleared 22 miles of carriage roads and walks in the surrounding woods. Of these, only the West Lawn Trail and Saw Kill Trail have been restored. (More will be rebuilt each year.)

The West Lawn Trail starts from the south side of the mansion between a double row of hemlocks. It descends around the edge of the grassy bowl, skirts the lily pond, and enters the North Woods, filled in spring with hepatica, red and white trillium, wild sarsaparilla, Solomon's-seal, and dog-tooth violet. The walk passes a small quarry, where the mansion's bluestone steps were cut, and eventually connects with the Saw Kill Trail.

A thick layer of bark carpets the Saw Kill Trail as it winds and angles down a steep hillside, through beech, red oaks, and hemlocks. Rough wood steps navigate the steepest "corners." Invasive ailanthus has been cleared from the woods, but felled trees and mammoth upturned roots remain, witness to the progression of a natural forest.

Halfway down the trail, you become aware of a low roar—like distant traffic—that grows stronger as you descend. At the bottom, like a reward, the falls of the Saw Kill River come into view. The water boils through a widening gorge, churning over huge boulders. Even in the dry days of summer, the water roils and rushes, a thoroughly satisfying cataract, well worth the climb back up the hill.

When General John Ross Delafield inherited Montgomery Place in 1921, his wife, Violetta, was already an amateur botanist. Her specialty was mushrooms. While General Delafield introduced plumbing to the mansion, Violetta cataloged all the flora in the North and South Woods and began the gardens that stretch from the mansion to the South Woods. She created the "rough" garden, the family's name for the rock and native plant garden; an ellipse of grass, trees, and water; herb and rose gardens; and perennial borders—all now under restoration.

The rough garden covers a large, shallow basin. Along one side, a stream trickles into pools and rills, over echo chambers built into the rocks. A web of flagstone paths weaves among a sprinkling of wood hyacinths, spiderworts, Canada lilies, and native ginger. Smaller paths spread out from the main ones until one section is more paths than plants. Tall junglelike stands of interrupted fern and clumps of sensitive fern cluster along the central path. In early spring thousands of snowdrops and winter aconite star the garden. Then come squill, bleeding-heart, trout lilies, and Virginia bluebells.

Violetta dug plants from the woods and installed them in her rough garden. One such is lizard's-tail (*Saururus cernuus*), now an endangered native species, which has happily taken over a large swampy patch of the garden.

All of these rough garden plants, dating from Violetta's time, were found when the garden recently was cleaned of four feet of nettles and weeds. Replanting will begin when research on the original plantings is completed. According to Julie Schaller, staff horticulturist, Violetta made that task a historian's dream by leaving a rich mine of records. "We have her original diagrams and planting notebook. We have copies of letters written to order plants and trees, plus all the invoices telling us what was purchased for where, when, at what price."

The main path of the rough garden leads to an apple-shaped flagstone "anteroom" that opens onto the ellipse. The simple pattern of the ellipse—a flat, oval pool set in an oval of grass, framed by a double row of hemlocks—makes it a tranquil respite after the "action" of the rough garden. Overhead, the treetops outline an oval patch of blue sky. Golden orange daylilies and rangy small-flowered white irises provide off-center interest, like a beauty mark, on one side of the pool.

Nearby, a wire archway leads to Violetta's ultraformal herb and rose gardens. The serpentine brick walks of the herb garden have been meticulously relaid. Bricks set vertically in sailor style (with the wide surface facing out—in soldier style, the narrow surface faces out) edge the beds that radiate from a central sundial. The design of this 35-by-50-foot garden is imposed by the formal brickwork. Culinary, medicinal, and decorative herbs, planted in formations as precise as the brick edging, will fill out and look more at ease as they mature.

The rose garden, half again as large as the herb garden, is bordered by low, full bushes of the Livingston rose. At least that's what the family called it. The real name for this old-fashioned hybrid perpetual rose is 'Marquise Bocella'. A good, rich pink with a unique ambrosial fragrance, the rose looks as if it were made from layers of tissue paper tightly wound into close, short petals.

Eventually, the garden will have all 1920s and 1930s roses and old-fashioned shrub roses, arranged by color in beds of yellow, pink, red, and white. Now, one shrub rose, the tall 'Father Hugo', stands in each section of the garden, bearing its open-petaled yellow blooms the last two weeks of May. Lilac hedges line two sides of the garden, and roses climb up a stone wall on another side.

79

Next to the rose and herb gardens is a charming stone cottage, which was Violetta's potting shed, and her greenhouse, newly rebuilt. The greenhouse may once again display a collection of African succulents similar to Violetta's, which was sent to the New York Botanical Garden in the 1940s. The greenhouse will also be used for propagation, especially of unusual plant varieties—like *Hydrangea paniculata*—found on the estate.

Nearby are perennial borders of iris, phlox, foxglove, delphinium, bee balm, bellflower, boltonia, and assorted lilies, lupines, and asters—all planted by Violetta 50 to 60 years ago. These borders too will be researched before replanting begins.

The paths in this part of the garden are deep with golden tan pebbles, the result of another kind of research. When restoration began, removal of an overgrowth of turf revealed pebbles from the old paths. The pebbles were sent to a geologist who determined that they could only have come from Long Island. The source was tracked down, and Long Island "grist" (its industry name) once more paves the paths.

Violetta created her varied and enchanting gardens in a landscape that originated with another remarkable woman, Janet Livingston Montgomery. Janet was 61 years old when she started building Montgomery Place in 1804. She was rich and well connected. A widow at 32—her husband, a general, had been killed in the Revolutionary War—she was long accustomed to managing her own affairs. Janet opened a commercial nursery on her property and advertised in Poughkeepsie newspapers to sell her apple, pear, and peach trees, the same varieties that now grow on either side of the mile-long drive to the mansion.

Janet Livingston Montgomery and her descendants never threw anything away. Almost 200 years of sales slips were found. Even pieces of the house that had fallen off were labeled, wrapped, and stored. The furniture in the mansion, collected over the decades, ranges in style from Federal to rococo revival; other objects, from arrowheads and Gilbert Stuart paintings to a game of pick-up-sticks shaped like little tools. The wallpapers alone—an interior garden of flowers and ribbons—are worth a visit, their colors as clear as though made today.

Historic Hudson Valley, a nonprofit museum of historic Hudson River sites, is restoring Montgomery Place. The museum bought the property in 1985 and has been, as Edward Livingston wrote about his activities in 1835, ". . . planting, cutting down, leveling, sloping, opening views, clearing walks, and preparing much work for the ensuing spring to embellish."

MONTGOMERY PLACE, River Road, PO Box 32, Annandale-on-Hudson, NY 12504. (914) 758-5461.

OPEN
Mansion and grounds, daily, except Tuesday, April through October, 10 A.M. to 5 P.M.; grounds, until sunset on summer weekends. Weekends only, November, December, and March. Closed January and February. Admission fee.

FACILITIES
· Picnicking permitted.
· Gift shop.
· Ramp to mansion; lawns and views accessible to people with physical disabilities; parts of the gardens have limited access.

EVENTS
· Games people used to play, provided free: croquet, French hoops, puzzles, chess, Parchesi, and Chinese checkers.
· Guided tours of mansion and grounds; times posted daily.
· Guided tours describing the restoration process and ongoing work, including a visit to the Coach House carpentry workshop; times posted daily.
· Pick-your-own apples in the orchards, in the fall.

DIRECTIONS
Henry Hudson Parkway to Saw Mill River Parkway to Taconic State Parkway. Take Pine Plains/Red Hook Exit (Route 199), and go west 10 miles on Route 199, through Red Hook, to Route 9G. Turn right on 9G, and go about 1 mile to Annandale Road; turn left and bear left at the green. Go about ¼ mile to the entrance of Montgomery Place on the right.

OLANA

HUDSON, NEW YORK

Olana was the country estate of Frederic Church, a leading artist of the Hudson River School of painting, who became famous depicting sublime wild, naturalistic American landscapes on vast canvasses.

Of all the sites that the nineteenth-century landed gentry chose for their country seats, none is more dramatic, compelling, or more achingly beautiful than Olana. It is the kind of landscape that Church frequently painted—romantic, expansive, monumental. Like the popular poem of the day, Olana is "America the Beautiful."

From its hilltop, Olana commands the grandest of panoramas. A saddleback cups a man-made lake fringed with trees. The sight line then descends to the Hudson River far below, a loop of gray satin that slips out of sight between steeply forested slopes. The Catskills recede into an endless horizon of blue.

Olana was Frederic Church's love. In 1867, after selling his painting *Heart of the Andes* for a record $10,000, Church purchased the first 126 acres of Olana, adding to them through the years. He built his Persian-style villa in 1872 and tinkered with the landscape until his death in 1900.

The broader landscape—all 250 acres of it—is the chief reason to visit Olana. Church composed a planned sequence of natural features: veiled glimpses of a valley, leafy tunnels, and panoramas. A road circled past the orchards and hayfields of his own working farm, then opened to views of farmlands and valleys to the east.

Only at the summit is the full glory of the Hudson River revealed. Sited just below the crest of the hill against a backdrop of trees, Olana is a Persian bonbon of turrets, domes, and Moorish arches that caps a 25-acre expanse of manicured lawn. The intent of such openness is clear: nothing should upstage the "grander canvas" of nature. The grounds surrounding a country house should be "modest and unobtrusive." Church took this concept to its limit. The immediate environs of the mansion are bare of flowering shrubs, formal gardens, or vines.

Below this naked expanse of lawn, but out of view of Olana's verandas, is a small crescent-shaped garden, a luxurious tangle of peonies, asters, irises, poppies, roses, and daylilies held in restraint by a curved stone wall and a fence. It is called the Mingled Garden and makes a focus for a pleasant downhill stroll.

The winding roads that lead to the summit have been changed since the state took ownership in 1966. But the three major carriage roads planned by Church can still be traversed on foot. That is a joy, as is the villa, whose exterior and interior spaces were so carefully sketched and color tinted by Church. Blue-, green-, pink-, and salmon-colored tiles are imbedded in the trim around windows, turrets, doorways, and Moorish arches. The colors of the central interior court—pale pinks, green, beige, and cool grays—are repeated throughout the house, furnished with Church's masterpieces, exotic woods, ceramics, fabrics, silver and gold artifacts from the Orient and India.

OLANA STATE HISTORIC SITE, RD 2, Hudson, New York 12534. (518) 828-0135.

OPEN
· House, May through October, Wednesday through Saturday, 10 A.M. to 4 P.M.; Sunday, 1 P.M. to 4 P.M., by guided tour only. Daily tickets are limited, so call in advance for reservations. After Labor Day, Wednesday through Saturday, noon to 4 P.M.; Sunday, 1 P.M. to 4 P.M. Closed Monday and Tuesday. Open Memorial Day, Fourth of July, and Labor Day. Admission fee.
· Grounds, daily, from 8 A.M. to sunset.

FACILITIES
· Picnicking.
· Facilities for wheelchairs.

EVENTS
Group tours by reservation only, 2 weeks in advance.

DIRECTIONS
Henry Hudson Parkway to Taconic State Parkway to Hudson exit. Take Route 23 west to Route 9G south. Olana is 5 miles south of the town of Hudson.

VANDERBILT MANSION ITALIAN GARDENS

HYDE PARK, NEW YORK

On the serpentine drive leading up to the Vanderbilt mansion, brick walls are the first thing you glimpse in the distance. Their intense red color—almost harsh—stretches starkly across the bright green landscape, an aberration, not an integral part of it. These are the century-old walls that surround the formal Italian Gardens. Even up close the walls have a nakedness—no vine or shrub or flower clothes them. They stand alone, a powerful frame for the gardens.

The gardens are worthy of such a frame. Built out of sight of the mansion, they cover almost two acres, terraced in eight levels. From the grassy entrance, your first sight is a tantalizing hint—two more grassy levels and the tops of a pergola, brick piers, and the tile roof of a pool house—not the full sweep of the gardens. The terraces are revealed bit by bit as you descend the hillside, 35 feet from top to bottom. Next come two levels of annuals, then a formal Italian perennial garden, and two levels of roses. Trellises, pools, a loggia, and the brick piers and walls embellish the gardens.

Frederick W. Vanderbilt, grandson of Commodore Vanderbilt, bought the estate in 1895 from the grandson of another tycoon, John Jacob Astor. At that time, the estate included a smaller garden on the present site and the brick walls, both at least two decades old.

The Vanderbilts hired New York landscape architect James L.

Greenleaf to redesign what was then the lowest level of the gardens in the Italian style, a fusion of art and nature. "Nature is not art," Greenleaf said, "nature is blind when it comes to handling things. . . ." So Greenleaf created a highly structured garden. A central walk connects the pergola at the head of the garden with the pool house at the end. The pillars of the pool house and the pergola roof—patterned like a spiderweb on the inside—are both beautifully crafted reconstructions in cypress.

The first part of the walk cuts on a slope between waist-high stone walls that buttress raised banks planted with cherry trees. Five-foot-wide borders, each with similar perennials, line the walk. In late spring, the wild color combinations of a few varieties supply the drama—swathes of fiery oriental poppies, free-form carpets of cerise dianthus, and great stands of hybrid lupines in full-flowering 15-inch spikes of rose, ruby, French vanilla, purple, and raspberry sherbert.

The walk then passes between large rectangles of perennials, bordered in spring with extraordinary clumps of columbines, their upturned five-inch flowers in delicious combinations of ruby and pale yellow, light salmon and yellow, lavender and cream. Nearby, the ground is a solid clear blue from the fallen petals of a large patch of flax. The beds are still full of color in fall, a time when the Vanderbilts were usually in residence. Yellow foxglove is in bloom, along with blue and white delphinium, white veronica and campanula, yellow and blue violas, chrysanthemums, and rich clumps of pink and white Japanese anemones.

Recently planted vines—trumpet, honeysuckle, and wisteria—in time will clothe the walls near the pool house. From its shade, a marble statue of a bathing maiden, *Barefoot Kate*, looks out over an empty pool, scheduled to be repaired and refilled by 1989.

On the upper terrace of annuals, blue salvias, red cannas, marigolds, and white petunias bloom in geometrically shaped beds. Red begonias spice the same mix of annuals on the next level, in beds with Rorschach-like shapes.

Graceful iron curlicues crown the brick walls that separate the formal perennial garden from the two-level rose garden, the last addition made by the Vanderbilts. Originally, vines covered the ironwork to conceal the gardens beyond, kept as a grand finale.

At the Vanderbilts' weekend house parties in early summer and fall, a tour of the gardens was part of the programmed entertainment, always ending with Japanese tea served in the pale pink loggia at the foot of the rose garden. Behind the loggia, a waterfall murmurs on Crum Elbow Creek.

Mr. Vanderbilt had a degree in horticulture from Yale, the first in his family to graduate from college. The gardens were his joy. After his wife's death, he spent more time at Hyde Park, often winning blue ribbons for flowers and vegetables at the Dutchess County Fair.

The Vanderbilts had no children. Mrs. Vanderbilt's niece inherited the estate, which she gave to the National Park Service in 1940.

During the war years, weeds took over. Vines as thick as a man's thigh had partially destroyed the walls and structures by the time the National Park Service began restoring them in 1974.

Reconstruction was completed in 1983, but the gardens would be a bare bones framework without the Frederick W. Vanderbilt Garden Association. This volunteer group begs, borrows, and cajoles to get money and materials for the garden. Members mow lawns, rake the gravel paths, sweep the stairs, trim and clip. Level by level, they have replanted the gardens as they existed when Vanderbilt died in 1938. (National Park Service policy is to maintain property as it was at the previous owner's death.)

They planted 4,000 perennials in 1986 and 1,000 donated rose bushes in 1987. In 1988 forty volunteers planted 6,000 annuals in three hours. Individual memorial plaques clutter the rose beds, but each brings money to buy benches, vines, ironwork, and arbors.

When Vanderbilt bought the property, it had already been a great country estate for well over a century. The Bard family, for whom Bard College is named, summered here. The next owner, physician and botanist David Hosack, purchased the estate in 1828. Hosack had already established a 20-acre botanical garden of medicinal plants in New York City on the site now occupied by Rockefeller Center. He hired André Parmentier, a Belgian who became renowned as one of America's first landscape gardeners and nurserymen. Together the two men created the foundation of the naturalistic parklike grounds that are the setting for the Vanderbilt mansion today.

The mansion, a massive limestone rectangle of 50 rooms, was designed by McKim, Mead, and White in the beaux arts style. Gray and stern outside, its interiors are lavishly decorated—marble and inlay, tapestries, gilt, gold leaf, and ormolu. Mrs. Vanderbilt's room, the epitome of *luxe*, is a reproduction of a queen's bedroom from the time of Louis XV, including the marble rail around the bed where courtiers would stand at the daily levees.

VANDERBILT MANSION ITALIAN GARDENS, Hyde Park, NY 12538. (914) 229-7770.

OPEN
- Grounds, daily, sunrise to sunset, except New Year's Day, Thanksgiving, and Christmas. No admission fee.
- Mansion, daily, April through October, tours every half hour, 10 A.M. to 5:30 P.M.; November through March, Thursday through Monday, 9:30 A.M. to 4:30 P.M. Reservations necessary for groups; call (914) 229-9115. Admission fee.

FACILITIES
- Picnicking permitted.
- Gift shop.
- Gardens not easily accessible to people with physical disabilities; mansion accessible to light wheelchairs.

EVENTS
- Concerts on the lawn (big band and pop music), every Wednesday night, June through mid-August. No admission fee.
- Antique car show, second Sunday in June. No admission fee.

DIRECTIONS
Henry Hudson Parkway to Saw Mill River Parkway, to Taconic State Parkway, to Route 55 west. Just before the Mid-Hudson Bridge across the Hudson River, turn right onto Route 9 north. Go about 6 miles, and the mansion is on the left.

NEW
JERSEY

COLONIAL PARK
ARBORETUM

EAST MILLSTONE, NEW JERSEY

❧ The reason to visit the Colonial Park Arboretum, 144 acres of specimen trees, dwarf conifers, flowering shrubs, and the Fragrance and Sensory Garden, is roses. Four thousand of them, in the Rudolf W. van der Goot Rose Garden.

Van der Goot, who became Somerset County's first horticulturist in 1968, spent seven years designing and planting the one-acre garden, which is in three sections.

The first section was created from the remnants of the formal garden of the Mettler Estate. (The Mettlers owned and farmed all the land that now makes up the Arboretum.) Using the old brick-edged beds and flagstone walks, van der Goot laid out a precise, symmetric garden. In each sharp-edged bed, a wide frame of blade-perfect grass surrounds hybrid tea and tree roses. In the center of this section, miniature roses encircle a small pool and fountain. One bed, called Grandmother's Garden, is fragrant with roses popular before World War II. Four beds are devoted to All-America Rose Selections winning roses.

As an official All-America Rose Selections (AARS) display garden, the van der Goot Garden receives four new winning rose varieties each year. AARS, a nonprofit trade association, makes its annual selection of prize roses from cultivars—all new to the United

States market—that have been grown for two years in one of 20 trial gardens throughout the country. In exchange for a promise to display the roses for three years, public gardens are then given the winning cultivars a year before they become commercially available.

Trellises of climbing roses frame the middle section of the garden. Paths of mellow red brick border beds of polyanthas and floribundas. Historic roses grow around the perimeter. Among them are the tightly petaled pink Bourbon rose 'Louise Odier' and the white and pink 'York-and-Lancaster', a sixteenth-century rose named for the opposing families in the War of the Roses.

More heritage roses and modern hybrids grow in the smaller third section of the garden, planted in formal Dutch-style beds edged with dwarf candytuft. The compact size of the beds permits a close view of each rose.

Next to the rose garden, the Fragrance and Sensory Garden is planted on top of waist-high stone walls so that braille labels are within easy reach. You can touch, sniff, even taste. The garden is a heady mix of smells—pineapple sage, hyssop, anise basil, chocolate mint, nutmeg geranium; and textures—velvety lamb's-ears and soft, hairy southernwood.

At the back of the touch-and-smell beds, large masses of perennials and annuals are planted in smashing combinations. In one corner, golden Dahlberg daisies mix brilliantly with scarlet snapdragons and 'Sunny Red' cosmos; in another, the cream-edged leaves of variegated daphne 'Carol Mackie' pair with spiky variegated yucca.

COLONIAL PARK ARBORETUM, RD 1, Mettler's Road, East Millstone, NJ 08873. (201) 873-2459.

OPEN
· Arboretum, daily, sunrise to half hour before sunset.
· Rudolf W. van der Goot Rose Garden and Fragrance and Sensory Garden, daily, Memorial Day weekend through Labor Day, 10 A.M. to 8 P.M.; after Labor Day through October 31, 10 A.M. to 4:30 P.M. One caveat: Visit the Rose Garden in June before the Japanese beetles arrive in July. No admission fee.

FACILITIES
· Picnicking permitted.
· Accessible to people with physical disabilities.
· Weddings can be held in the Arboretum (no fee) and photographs

taken in the Rose Garden (fee). Permit needed for both; call (201) 234-2677.

EVENTS

- Rose Day, first Saturday in June, 10 A.M. to 2 P.M., sale of plants, slide show, lectures, clinics; light refreshments available. No admission fee.
- Herb Day, second Saturday in July, 10 A.M. to 3 P.M., sale of herb plants, lectures. No admission fee.

DIRECTIONS

Lincoln Tunnel to New Jersey Turnpike south to Exit 10 to I-287 north. From I-287, take Exit 7 at Weston Canal Road. Go south on Weston Canal Road. Do not cross Weston Causeway, but turn left and continue along the canal until the road turns left onto Weston Road. Take the first right onto Mettler's Road. The Arboretum is about 1 mile ahead on the right.

DUKE GARDENS

SOMERVILLE, NEW JERSEY

It's impossible not to gasp at the first mass of color, flowering trees, marble statuary, and the forest of greenery as you step through the greenhouse entrance to Duke Gardens. A warmed fragrance immediately envelops you.

Eleven garden "rooms" unfold under an acre of glass. This is not a botanical garden; nothing is labeled. But Duke Gardens is grand visual entertainment, good for the winter blahs or a wilted spirit in any season.

The 11 gardens were laid out by different landscape designers but always under the firm hand and aesthetic eye of Doris Duke, the American Tobacco Company heiress. The gardens were, after all, a reflection of her travels and knowledge of gardens around the world. "There was no budget," said Jerry Eaton, Duke Gardens' first director. "It cost what it had to cost—we bought what we needed; it was done well. Miss Duke knew what she wanted."

Billed as "perfection under glass," each room is defined by era, climate, or country, although the plants aren't always botanically consistent with the theme. The rooms are as Miss Duke defined them originally:

The Italian Garden is airy, with feathery acacia and mimosa trees. The Colonial Garden blooms with hydrangea, camellias, and a luxuriant plumbago vine. The Edwardian Garden is a hothouse of conservatory palms, ferns, and orchids. The Desert Garden shows a monumental century plant and cacti. The Chinese Garden is an oasis of weeping willows and weeping jasmine overhanging a frog-filled lily pond. The Japanese Garden displays trees and shrubs that have been layered, sculptured, espaliered, and bonsaied. The Tropical and Subtropical gardens are a mix of the common and the rare, from houseplants to tree ferns.

But the grandest spectacles are the French, English, and Indo-Persian gardens.

The French Garden is a forest stage set. Woodland light filters through dark green latticework that covers walls, barrel-vaulted roof, pillars, and beams. Ropes of ivy around the pillars and along the beams intensify the greenness. Within this verdant container are parterres. Miniature hedges of boxwood and ilex outline intricate fleur-de-lis patterns filled with satiny tulips of white, eggplant, crimson, and gold. The structure of this garden is a truly dramatic creation.

The Indo-Persian Garden is the most exotic of all and needs only a white-robed sheik to complete the romance. As in every Persian garden, water is the backbone. A straight and narrow water channel flows down the center, transversed by a shorter channel that forms a cross of water. Gravity fed, the water flows through three levels, each level defined by white filigreed screens and a change in plantings. In the first level, perfectly pruned citrus trees, like large green lollipops, alternate with pencil-thin cypresses. Each tree is set in a star-shaped bed planted with grape hyacinths or blue, purple, or yellow pansies. In the middle level, papaya trees grow alongside large ixora shrubs, gorgeous for the orange-fuchsia-red color of their blossoms. In the third level, a white fountain bubbles at the point where the water channels cross, starting the water on its way the length of the garden. The channels set off squares of white cement planted with fat white and red roses, a flower much beloved by Persians.

The English Garden has double impact: a dramatic vista and herbaceous borders in vivid colors. The vista runs the 75-foot length of the garden, between the borders, ending at a treelike topiary ball at the far end. The borders are dazzling—wide beds of white stock, lavender cleome, pink and yellow snapdragons, cosmos, marigolds, blue scabiosa, tulips, ageratum, strawflowers, orange Enchantment lilies, and purple statice. Hardly the classic English perennial border but each plant is in full bloom and each bloom in perfect condition. The topiary turns out to be, on close inspection, a green ball of succulents atop a "trunk" planted in a stone urn supported by stone cherubs. Spread out on the ground around the cherubs is a sunburst pattern of blue, gray, and green succulents—10 feet across—bedded in sparkling white crushed marble. The entire assemblage is encircled by a three-inch-high edging of bright green crassula.

At Duke Gardens, visitors must take a guided tour. The pace is fast—11 gardens in 45 minutes. You cannot wander off to look at a special shrub or pause at length in front of a particularly glorious blossom. For a serious gardener, this can produce a high level of frustration.

Duke Gardens comprises only 60 acres of the grand 2,300-acre estate James Buchanan Duke created at the end of the nineteenth century when he was president of the American Tobacco Company. He imported architects and stone masons, had lagoons dug out, built greenhouses and fountains. When he died in 1925, Duke left the estate to his only child, 13-year-old Doris.

In 1958 when Miss Duke decided to create these international gardens, the greenhouses stood empty. Her task was immense. It took six years to clear rubble, rebuild structures, install the complex heating and watering systems necessary to sustain many different climates, and design and build the 11 gardens to Miss Duke's perfectionist standards. If she didn't like the way a garden looked, she had it torn out. Gardeners and designers started all over again. When the gardens were finally "right," Miss Duke opened them to the public in 1964.

While the gardens are public, the estate is very private. When not in Hawaii or Newport or traveling, Miss Duke lives here in the mansion her father built, complete with indoor swimming pool and bowling alleys.

DUKE GARDENS FOUNDATION, INC., Somerville, NJ 08876. (201) 722-3700.

OPEN
Daily, October through May, noon to 4 P.M.; closed Thanksgiving, Christmas, New Year's Day. Reservations required. Admission fee.

DIRECTIONS
Lincoln Tunnel to New Jersey Turnpike south to Exit 10 to I-287 north, to Route 22 west, to Route 206 south. About 1¼ miles past Somerset Shopping Center, Duke is on the right.

LEONARD J. BUCK GARDEN

FAR HILLS, NEW JERSEY

In this rocky, narrow gorge, unceremoniously called Moggy Hollow, there is a touch of magic. It is a place where the wild things are. A deep green river of grass flows around rocky outcroppings crouched as if ready to spring to life with the right touch.

It's hard to keep your hands off these rock sculptures. Some are a deep plum color and some a chocolate brown, with welts of green velvety moss oozing from fissures. Others are charcoal gray, shot with hundreds of blackened holes made by escaping gasses from volcanic eruptions millions of years ago.

You enter this place of magic on a graveled path that loops the gorge in a figure eight, winding around the outcroppings, which vary in size and shape. Some are 50 feet high, some 80 feet long, some the size of a footstool. Each rock has been given a name, although they are hard to identify, because they bear no labels and the paths weave through, around, and on top of the outcroppings.

Each is a separate garden with its own microclimate and plantings. Rock ledges are covered with ferns and succulents. Crowns of pink columbine and arbutus trail down cliffs. Wildflowers bedazzle. Woodsy smells of mint, cinnamon, moist earth, honeysuckle, and pine mingle in this verdant, humid valley.

This 15-acre cul-de-sac is a rock gardener's paradise, where rock ledges and walls span 175,000,000 years of geological history. The outcroppings are primarily basalt, boiled out of the earth as molten lava by a volcano long before the Wisconsin ice sheet (15,000 years ago) and waterfalls from an ancient lake (11,000 years ago) scoured out the rest of the gorge.

Near the entrance to the gorge, the first outcropping is Big Rock, shaped like a dinosaur, tail and all. Campanulas creep up from the base, and moss creeps down from the top. Half-domes of sea-foam green sedum cluster in a shallow of the rock, which turns a deep burgundy color in the late afternoon sun. Other sedums—pearly green, mint green, yellow, and white—spread runners of color along Big Rock. Columbines, geraniums, gold stars, beds of long-stemmed white violets, and sweet woodruff border the path.

Next on the rock safari, Horseshoe Rock, green with trees and plants, is a relict shaped by some primordial waterfall, its broad, flat pate worn smooth by the billions of gallons of water that once flowed over it. The top is now sunbaked and dry, home to nests of hens-and-chickens, members of the cactus family, sempervivums, and succulents in shades of pale green and wine red. These succulents are true sufferers, able to thrive best in drought conditions and acidic, gravelly soil. Ordinarily rocks are alkaline, but companion mosses on Horseshoe Rock provide the acid that the succulents need to survive. Blueberries, heaths, and heathers (heaths usually bloom in winter, heathers in summer) fringe the base in a delicate array of pink, dusty gold, olive, and lemon green.

The path crosses Moggy Brook to Polypoda Rock, so named for the six-inch-tall leathery ferns that grow on the upper ledges. Polypoda Rock is a creation of both man and nature. The upper half is a natural cliff that runs 80 feet in length. The lower half is made of rock slabs laid horizontally to create pockets of soil that now support junipers and azaleas. Beginning each March, adonis, celandines, buttercups, and meadow rues streak Polypoda with yellow. In June yellow lady's-slipper, a dainty wild orchid that resists propagation, comes to life, followed by a colony of feathery white foamflowers.

Next, exposed to much sun and wind, comes Reno Rock, brightened with mantles of helianthemums, cowslips, alliums, and penstemons. New Rock (really the backside of Horseshoe Rock) harbors shade lovers like Solomon's-plume and the somber mosslike saxifrages and androsaces.

Little Rock (with little sun) burrows in beds of bleeding-heart, ferns, pinks, wild columbine, sweet woodruff, and epimedium.

And so the outcroppings proceed up the valley, 13 in all, looking as if nature had bestowed her most brilliant adornments on each rock. Nature did not.

The garden is the creation of a 40-year partnership between the late Leonard J. Buck, a mining engineer, and Zenon Schreiber, a Swiss-born landscape architect, now retired, who specialized in alpine plantings and rock gardens.

Buck, a trustee of the New York Botanical Garden and a director of the American Rock Garden Society, purchased the valley as part of a 50-acre country estate in 1934. Long fascinated by the relationship between plants and mineral deposits, he wanted to create an ecologically correct garden that would not look man-made. He first met Schreiber tending his rock garden display at a New York flower show and invited him to the valley. The lure was irresistible to Schreiber; the partnership began. When the two started their garden, only one rock formation was visible. The others were buried under loose traprock.

They went to work with chisels, crowbars, and dynamite, clearing and sculpting rocks to fit their aesthetic vision, accenting horizontal effects. Meticulously, they placed each planting in its appropriate microclimatic niche.

Buck and Schreiber linked their outcroppings to other microclimates they created. They dammed Moggy Brook with log-stepped waterfalls, creating a small swamp, bog, and pond. They embellished the stream banks with maidenhair fern and the pond with blue-green blades of elegant giant irises. They walled a meadow with azaleas and rhododendrons, carved out open lawns for vistas. So discerning was their vision that the original natural ravine is now a unity of rock, alpine and woody plants, wildflowers, and a forest of beech, linden, hornbeam, hemlock, and oak.

Buck died in 1974. Two years later his widow, Helen, donated the garden, 33 acres in all, to the Somerset County Park Commission. Most plants are labeled. A heather and perennial garden and dwarf conifers have been planted near the Visitors Center.

LEONARD J. BUCK GARDEN, R.D. 2, Layton Road, Far Hills, NJ 07931-9802. (201) 234-2677.

OPEN
· Daily, Monday through Saturday, 10 A.M. to 4 P.M.; Sunday, noon to 5 P.M.; in winter, noon to 4 P.M. Closed New Year's Day, Thanksgiving, and Christmas, and if weather conditions are hazardous. No admission fee.

FACILITIES
Very limited accessibility to people with physical disabilities; gravel paths and steps.

EVENTS
· Periodic slide shows, lectures on rock gardening and horticulture.
· Group tours available for 8 persons or more, with advance reservations.

DIRECTIONS
Lincoln Tunnel to New Jersey Turnpike south to Exit 14 (before Newark Airport). Take Route 78 west toward Morristown for 28 miles to Route 287 north. Go about 3 miles on Route 287 to Exit 18B. Take Route 206 north. When road splits, take Route 202 north. Go through town of Bedminster. At blinker, make a right turn onto an unmarked road called Liberty Corner Road, and go 1 mile. Turn right onto Layton Road. Garden is second drive on the left.

REEVES-REED
ARBORETUM

SUMMIT, NEW JERSEY

In the middle of an upper-class neighborhood of very large, very old, and very well kept houses is a 12½-acre jewel, Reeves-Reed Arboretum. Standing in front of the mansion, which sits on a rise, you can see most of the Arboretum spread before you: a kettle; a perennial border; rose, herb, and azalea gardens; lawns; and the woodlands beyond. Starting at stone steps flanked by two cherry trees, one weeping, one Japanese, the vista extends past a giant redwood, down a sweep of green lawn to two monumental rhododendrons that mark a path into the woods.

From the mansion, elevated as it is, you look into the top two-thirds of the trees. From this vantage point, the depth of foliage has an immediacy that gives the feeling of being in a tree house. In the golds, orange-reds, and mahoganies of fall, the trees appear layered against each other, the leaves of each discrete from its neighbor's.

No matter what the season, the kettle in front of the mansion is an astonishing sight. Whether bright with flowers, all green with foliage, or blanketed with snow, it startles the senses. A mammoth, steep-sided pothole, 28 feet deep and covering almost an acre, the kettle was formed from the melting of a chunk of glacial ice. In spring, thousands of daffodils turn it into a deep bowl of butter yellow. In summer, field flowers—bachelor's-buttons, coreopsis, oxeye daisies, black-eyed Susans, and red clover—spread a haze of color.

Between the kettle and the mansion, a two-level, serpentine perennial border blooms continuously from April on. In fall, the usual lavender, rose, maroon, and yellow of chrysanthemums are enriched by balloon flowers, rusty sedum 'Autumn Joy', Nippon daisies, a garish pink phlox, purple salvia, and the pure blue of plumbago. More lavender, rose, and purple are repeated in bushy asters.

Huge lustrous yellow- and red-berried hollies flank the side steps and front door of the mansion. On one side of the building, low stone walls, stone steps, and narrow pathways mingle their way down the slope, forming nooks and crannies. A collection of ferns and primulas borders a deeply shaded path. Another path shortcuts under the fragrant fleecy white panicles of a fringe tree (Chionanthus virginicus) and ends near a small rock-rimmed pool.

Nearby, the rose garden contains a number of the original hybrid teas, like 'Mirandy', 'Lowell Thomas', and 'Mrs. DuPont', that were planted in the 1920s. Because of the current interest in old-fashioned roses, the Arboretum has added a new garden of them: the pink and white 'York-and-Lancaster', dating from 1551, and the white single 'Blanc de Coubert', from the rugosa family, which also dates from the Middle Ages. Several, such as the pink 'Comte de Chambord', which flowers all summer, and the white and pink 'Alfred de Dalmas', a rare hybrid moss rose, are from the mid-1800s.

Many of the Arboretum's magnificent trees were here before the brown-shingle mansion was built in 1889. Black walnut, black oak, white oak, and American beech line the driveway. Among the indigenous maple, dogwood, hemlock, cedar, tulip, and spruce are three southern imports—a silver-bell tree (Halesia carolina), its branches lined with white bell-like flowers in spring; a yellowwood (Cladrastis lutea); and a glossy, large-leaved bull bay (Magnolia grandiflora). For many years, the bull bay was swaddled in burlap each winter for protection. It has now

❧

PRECEDING PAGE: *The kettle hole in front of the*
Reeves-Reed mansion.

grown too large to wrap but manages to survive the winter winds only slightly damaged.

A natural hardwood forest takes up the back section of Reeves-Reed. Here is a second kettle, this one almost 60 feet deep, where mayapples, ferns, wild geraniums, Jack-in-the-pulpits, and celandines grow in the shade. Walking the trails that crisscross the forest is like a journey through backwoods country—until clipped and trimmed suburban backyards come into sudden view. They are not so much an intrusion as a reason to appreciate even more the existence of the Arboretum.

Reeves-Reed, which takes its name from the two previous owners, was slated to be sold for development, when a group of neighbors asked the city of Summit to match half the purchase price. The city agreed, and the neighbors raised the other half. Reeves-Reed opened to the public in 1974 and is supported entirely by its membership.

REEVES-REED ARBORETUM, 165 Hobart Avenue, Summit, NJ 07901. (201) 273-8787. Owned by the city of Summit.

OPEN
- Grounds, daily, during daylight hours. No admission fee.
- Office, Monday, Tuesday, and Thursday, 9 A.M. to 3 P.M.

FACILITIES
Ramps for people with physical disabilities; paved and grass paths.

EVENTS
- Easter sunrise service, 5:30 A.M., ecumenical service conducted outdoors; coffee served afterward. No admission fee.
- Rose Day, a Sunday in June; rose experts available to answer questions. No admission fee.
- Petals and Pops, a September evening lawn concert. Admission fee.
- Harvest Festival, October, 10 A.M. to 4 P.M., entertainment, crafts, storytelling, music, demonstrations, food. No admission fee.
- Workshops and lectures throughout the year on horticultural and plant craft subjects. Admission fee.

DIRECTIONS
Lincoln Tunnel to New Jersey Turnpike to Exit 14. Take I-78 west to Exit 48 (Springfield/Millburn) to Route 24 west. From Route 24 (parallel to Route 124), take Hobart Avenue exit; go left over the bridge and continue straight through the light. Up the hill on the left is the entrance sign for Reeves-Reed.

SKYLANDS
BOTANICAL
GARDEN

RINGWOOD, NEW JERSEY

At first sight, Skylands looks more like the great country estate it once was than what it is today—New Jersey's official botanical garden. None of the earmarks of an institution is present. The driveway is open. No signs direct your step. You might see women in wide-brimmed straw hats and floral-printed chiffons on a terrace, or little girls skipping by in shiny new Mary Janes. This is not a vision of some weekend house party of the thirties but one of the many wedding receptions now held here.

But Skylands is very much a botanical garden. On these 125 acres, about 5,000 varieties of plants grow in formal and informal gardens, including a Winter Garden; Terrace Gardens; annual and perennial gardens; rhododendron, heather, bog, and wildflower gardens; shrub and lilac collections; and a Crab Apple Vista.

The botanical riches are the legacy of Clarence McKenzie Lewis, an investment banker who for 30 years, beginning in the 1920s, collected plants from exotic locales like Afghanistan, New Zealand, and Chile and from nearby New Jersey roadsides and Pine Barrens. Whatever a plant's home climate, Lewis would try to grow it in New Jersey if he thought it had the slightest chance of surviving. His horticultural interests were so extensive that Skylands was registered as a plant nursery and inspected regularly by the U.S. Department of Agriculture.

Lewis's Tudor manor house, built from granite quarried on the estate, stretches across the top of a slight knoll. With its leaded windows and crenellated walls, it looks like nothing so much as a Princeton eating club.

From the manor house, Lewis could look out at what he called his Winter Garden—masses of evergreens growing in great island chains on either side of the front lawn. There are Japanese red pine, Atlas cedar, upright and weeping European beeches, plum yew, blue spruce, balsam fir and Algerian fir—30 varieties in all. The trees are planted close together but with enough room to walk around them.

The forms and textures of these full-grown specimens are extraordinarily beautiful. One tree has branches down to the ground; another has a solid mass of foliage shaped like a gumdrop that begins six feet up. The strong conical shape of a Japanese umbrella pine stands near the curving branches of a weeping beech. The colors of the evergreens—dusty gray, gray-blue and green-blue, red, gold and yellow, and all shades of green—indeed make a garden to cheer the spirit in winter.

In the formal Terrace Gardens, the feeling of elegance intensifies as garden follows garden. They descend in a straight line from the back of the manor house: Octagonal Garden, Magnolia Walk, Azalea Garden, Summer Garden, and Peony Garden. Each is a separate room, set within random plantings of tall evergreens.

In the Octagonal Garden, dwarf shrubs and small plants grow on top of a waist-high stone wall around a central pool and bronze fountain. In spring, primulas range in color from pale peach and yellow to bright orange-red, and a large clump of *Anemone nemorosa* opens its fresh lavender petals. The water for the pool and fountain—and for the other pools in the Terrace Gardens—comes down in six-inch cast-iron pipes from reservoirs Lewis had built six miles away in the Ramapo Mountains that rise above Skylands.

The Magnolia Walk is an opulent passageway, almost 300 feet long and 65 feet wide. Flagstone paths on either side of a grassy center are lined with sweet bay magnolias that bloom in June, creamy white and intensely fragrant. Hostas grow under the trees. Viburnum, honeysuckle, and daphne add their perfumes.

In the peaceful Azalea Garden, a wide channel of water runs between grass borders and banks of azaleas, spilling into a pool in the Summer Garden below. Here daylilies in fiery colors are framed by shoulder-high yew hedges. In the background, the limbs of Norway spruce make great swooping curves, the needles hanging down like fringe.

The last in the chain of Terrace Gardens is the Peony Garden, a broad aisle of grass, lined by tree peonies, known in their native China as the King of Flowers. But the most striking part of this garden is the exedra, a semicircular stone bench, set at the end in a circle of hemlocks. Solid stone down to the ground, this 25-foot-wide arc, the width of the grassy aisle, was intended to be a suitable monument for the family ashes, but they were never placed in the small vaults built into either side. Sitting on the bench, you can look back through the progression of gardens and see a part of the manor house.

Outside the Peony Garden, the lilac collection, 60 varieties in all, is casually set out in close quarters. So is the nearby shrub border, where the snowy blooms of a sorbaria quiver—the bush actually shakes—with hundreds of bees in July.

All of these gardens are on one side of Maple Avenue, a paved road that cuts through the estate. Young oaks recently replaced the ailing maples that lined the roadway, but the name remains. From the road, the land slopes down to a vast meadow, then to woods, before rising to the Ramapo Mountains beyond.

Just off the road, parterres of annuals occupy a spacious garden—about 200 feet square—enclosed by yew hedges. A stone bench marks each corner, and at the center, a large and ancient Greek stone wellhead formalizes this neat and proper garden. The annuals change every year and are not repeated for at least five years. Sometimes the beds are mixed, sometimes planted with a single variety, but always the color is vivid and strong. All the annuals are grown from seed in the greenhouse. Because Skylands can't take chances with germination and flowering, only tried and true varieties are grown.

The backbone of Skylands—the Crab Apple Vista—marks the boundary between the formal gardens and the informal gardens, meadow, and woods. A double line of crab apples, 166 trees in all, extends from a Tudor-style outbuilding called the Lodge, down the great meadow, to four weatherworn stone statues standing in a semicircle at the edge of the woods, a half-mile away. Eight-foot trees were planted in 1987 to recreate the original Vista that had died from age and neglect. Even in its adolescent state, the Vista by sheer length is an impressive sight.

The informal gardens merge one into the other. The approach is gradual: first the rhododendron garden, where a border of columbines grows so thickly that the plants push up between the slats of a curved wood bench. This garden is permanently fenced to keep out the deer, an omnipresent problem. Head landscape architect Hans Bussink tried all the recommended remedies from chemicals to human hair. None worked, so now his crew of four spends the entire month of November putting up miles of additional fencing around at-risk plantings.

The heather garden in spring is a delicious mix of yellow, green, purple, and white—chartreuse euphorbia, cypress, creeping thyme, hellebore, cotoneaster, candytuft, dwarf iris, pulmonaria, and, fitting right in, giant dandelions.

Down a path between shoulder-high walls of grasses and wildflowers is a bog garden and a pond covered with a solid film of apple green duckweed. A large frog sits motionless in the path, a perfect color match.

On a burning July day, the wildflower garden is cool under tall white pines. A stream slips through the garden, bridged by huge granite slabs. The path crosses and recrosses the stream, then winds in loops around boulders. In spring, the snug whorls of fiddleheads begin to unwind. Tiny spring beauties, primulas in tight red bud, gold thread, and Jack-in-the-pulpit bloom near tall stands of dark red and white trillium. The light green heart-shaped leaves of epimedium spread in the shade. Its delicate flower matches the pale maroon edging of the leaf. Bussink claims epimedium is the best ground cover of all—it grows well anywhere, even under beeches, Norway maples, and lindens. The only drawback is its comparatively high cost.

Summer wildflower beauties are scarlet berries of bunchberry, 30 kinds of ferns, the yellow pealike flowers of Dyer's greenwood, and a single Peruvian lily. One Canada lily stands six feet tall in a spot of sunlight, its orange flowers hanging in tiers like a giant chandelier.

Next to the wildflower garden is the Swan Pond, abandoned long ago by swans. Now, two Canada geese glide slowly in tandem, three fluff-ball goslings crowded between them. Only the sound of a rushing stream and the *plop* of frogs diving off the rocks break the quiet.

After Lewis sold Skylands in 1956, 2 gardeners replaced the 60 Lewis employed. By the time the state bought the place in 1966, it was a jungle. Restoration has proceeded slowly ever since. At this point, almost nothing is labeled, which can be maddening for the plant lover.

A volunteer group, the Skylands Association, has been responsible for much of the current revitalization. Members maintain eight of the gardens, operate the visitors' center, and badger the state for funds. Their efforts achieved a minor miracle in 1987, a $300,000 addition to the annual budget.

But Bussink tells a cautionary budget tale. "When I came to Skylands in 1968, it was healthy. But I was young and foolish and thought I knew it all, so I sprayed. When the state cut my budget, I stopped spraying, and insect damage was fierce for the next two years. Now, for the last five years, we don't spray and we don't get damage—nature restored its balance."

SKYLANDS BOTANICAL GARDEN, Ringwood State Park, PO Box 1304, Ringwood, NJ 07456. (201) 962-7031.

OPEN
Garden, daily, dawn to dusk. (Manor house closed to the public.) Rubber boots and insect repellent are needed in the informal gardens in spring. Admission fee on weekends, Memorial Day to Labor Day.

FACILITIES
Limited access to people with physical disabilities; steps in Terrace Gardens; grass paths.

EVENTS
· Two-day plant sale, first weekend in May.
· Skylands Association sponsors a variety of classes, spring through fall, on horticulture, nature photography, nature watercolor painting, etc.; call (201) 962-7525 or (201) 962-9534 (machine) for information. Admission fee.

DIRECTIONS
George Washington Bridge to Route 4 west to Route 208 north to the end. This becomes one lane; continue straight, crossing a bridge. After the bridge, take the first right turn onto Skyline Drive to the end. Turn right onto Route 511, and go to the second right, Sloatsburg Road (sign to Ringwood State Park). Go about 4½ miles to Morris Road (sign to Skylands Botanical Garden) and turn right. Skylands is at the end of the road.

WELL-SWEEP
HERB FARM

PORT MURRAY, NEW JERSEY

On a backcountry road, a picket fence fronts a picture postcard working farm—gardens, barn, chicken coops, greenhouse, and two acres of flowers. This is Well-Sweep Herb Farm, the home and business of Louise and Cyrus Hyde.

The Hydes raise some 600 varieties of herbs—100 thymes, 80 scented-leaf geraniums, and 40 rosemaries alone. Most grow in the display garden—in curved and sharp-angled beds, in standard topiaries, and in an elaborate Elizabethan knot garden—all framed by wide paths of soft-colored old brick.

The pattern of the knot garden jumps out in shades of green—light green dwarf hyssop, gray-green lavender, dark green germander—and crimson pigmy barberry. The standard topiaries are round balls of lemon and licorice verbena on slender four-foot trunks. More topiaries, of

'Logee Blue' rosemary, punctuate a bed crisscrossed with germander.

Much is old-fashioned here, as befits a garden whose plants have been used through the centuries for food, medicine, dye, or fragrance. Herb beds are separated by high hedges of Belladonna damask roses. The family makes jam from the petals. An iron bell hangs by the back door next to a sign, RING FOR SERVICE. A tire swing hangs from the huge maple that shades the terrace behind the house. At the end of a long brick path, a pint-sized building topped with a cupola shines with fresh sage green paint; it is a working three-hole privy.

A gravel path winds through plantings of orange and yellow lilies, phlox in three shades of pink, black-eyed Susans, golden yarrow, and purple coneflowers. In the cutting garden, Mrs. Hyde gathers a weekly bouquet for her church. "I hate cutting flowers," she says, "but having something called a cutting garden somehow makes it easier."

Old names and old stories sprinkle a tour of the garden with Mr. Hyde. He points out aconite, or wolfsbane. The dried roots were hung on medieval doors to keep away werewolves. Woad yields a blue dye that ancient Picts painted on their bodies before battle because it is a coagulant that stops bleeding. He breaks off a piece of horsetail grass, a prehistoric plant with a rough, ridged stem, to show how it can be used as a nail file.

Herbal remedies were part of the household where Mr. Hyde grew up. His mother used boneset (*Eupatorium perfoliatum*) in spring as a tonic. ("Very bitter, it was awful!") Joe-Pye weed reduced fever.

The herb Mr. Hyde uses medicinally more than any other is plantain, or buckhorn (*Plantago lanceolata*), viewed as a weed in most yards. While he doesn't prescribe it for others, here's what he does for poison ivy. He soaks large plantain leaves in hot water and damp-dries them. While they are drying, he takes a hot shower and scratches open the poison ivy blisters. He then swabs them with alcohol and squeezes the juice from the leaves onto the rash. "I go to bed, and the poison ivy is usually gone by morning," he says.

When Mr. Hyde began collecting herbs 30 years ago, it was hard to find seeds or cuttings. His main source was trading with other collectors, especially world travelers who gathered cuttings wherever they went. He still collects—right now he's on the trail of salt basil from Brazil. Drops of water form on the leaf in early morning and later crystallize into a salt—Mr. Hyde has been told—that people on salt-free

؞

PRECEDING PAGE: *Standard verbena and rosemary topiaries frame the Elizabethan knot garden.*

110

diets can use. Sometimes he collects closer to home: Uncle Chichi's tomato, "from my sister's husband's uncle." It looks like a long, boxy pepper and tastes delicious.

What began as a hobby became a sideline selling herbs and dried flowers. One of Mr. Hyde's customers was Waterloo Village, a colonial restoration in Stanhope, New Jersey. In time, he designed the herb garden for the village and became its full-time herbalist.

In 1967 the Hydes bought Well-Sweep with the idea of expanding their herb business. They cleared the woods, raised horses, sheep, pigs, and chickens, and added all the manure to the red-clay soil. They still do. After 20 years, the soil is good.

Mr. Hyde grows the plants, and Mrs. Hyde sells them. Most of the dried flowers in the gift shop—liatris, globe thistle, cockscomb, globe amaranth (*Gomphrena globosa*), and more—are grown on Well-Sweep's two back acres. The rest are gathered by Mr. Hyde on wildflower expeditions all over New Jersey and New York.

Mr. Hyde didn't plan it, but the chickens he breeds for show have turned into a business too. These are not basic barnyard chickens but long-tailed Japanese phoenix that sell for $150 a rooster; big buff cochins, 2½-feet tall, with feathers on their feet like pantaloons; and araucana from Chile, which lay blue and green eggs.

Well-Sweep is now a full-time business, about a third mail order and some wholesale. But most customers drive to this western outpost of New Jersey, drawn by what Allen Lacy in his *New York Times* garden column has called the best herb source in the East.

WELL-SWEEP HERB FARM, 317 Mt. Bethel Road, Port Murray, NJ 07865. (201) 852-5390.

OPEN
May through September, Tuesday through Saturday, except holidays, 9:30 A.M. to 5 P.M.; October through April—call ahead. Admission fee for group tours only, May through October.

FACILITIES
· Picnicking permitted.
· Gift shop.
· Accessible to people with physical disabilities; brick paths.

EVENTS
Two open houses, one in June and one in September; craftsmen (sundial and basket makers, quilters), lecture tours, demonstrations, refreshments, lunch.

DIRECTIONS

Lincoln Tunnel to Route 3 west to Route 46 west to Route 80 west to Exit 19. Go south on Route 517 to Hackettstown; pick up Route 46. Go right on Route 46 1 mile to Russling Road (at the Best Fruit Farm sign). Go left on Russling Road to the first intersection with a small island. Go left on Barker's Mill Road 1 block. Turn right onto Mt. Bethel Road. Well-Sweep is about 2 miles on the right.

PENNSYLVANIA AND DELAWARE VALLEY

ANDALUSIA

Andalusia—gardens and house—is understated elegance, a perfection of taste and maintenance, and the country seat of the Biddles of Philadelphia since 1814.

Set in lawns that roll down to the placid Delaware River, the Greek Revival country house is filled with sunlight, river breezes, and mementos—antiques, family portraits, and photographs of six generations of this remarkable family.

The house and gardens are historical site visiting at its best. The presence of the family that created them is so pervasive, you wonder: Have they all just gone downriver for tea?

The gardens are remnants of history. There is the dramatic, monasticlike garden called the Graperies; a twentieth-century Green Walk, splashy with annuals and conifers; a hay meadow with vistas that reach into a pruned forest of tulip trees, oaks, and beeches. Underneath these giants, dogwoods and azaleas bloom in a froth of white and pink in springtime. A romantic Gothic grotto sits at the river's edge.

Nicholas Biddle was a worldly and witty 25-year-old lawyer when he married Jane Craig, a rich, painfully shy 18-year-old. "My lady," Nicholas was to call her. Theirs was an enduring, happy marriage for 33 years. Jane once wrote, after 20 years of marriage, "I often feel that without you the world would be a blank to me."

In 1814 Nicholas bought the Craig family farm outside Philadelphia, which included a square, Regency-style house, for $17,000. The young couple proceeded to convert the house to the then-in-vogue Greek Revival style, more suitable to the emerging republic, busy tailoring its fashions and democratic precepts after ancient Greece.

Like many rich, educated gentlemen of his day, Nicholas Biddle was a horticulturist. In hopes of making a fortune in the silk trade, he planted 7,000 mulberry trees, *Morus alba multicaulis*, for the silkworms to feed on.

The mulberry trees proved to be a financial disaster, but the Graperies in time were not. Biddle planted Black Hamburg, Arvergnat, Muscatelle, and Meunier vines from Europe. To "acclimate so delicate a foreign plant" to the inhospitable climate of Pennsylvania, the iron-minded Biddle spared no efforts. He built two freestanding walls, each 100 feet long and 30 feet high. He espaliered the young grapevines along the southern side of the walls and enclosed them with sheets of glass, making a right-triangled "forcing house." With the installation of furnaces in his triangular glass shed, he created one of the first greenhouses in America.

The cost was enormous—$21,000, which today translates into $200,000. After six years, Biddle was able to report to his cousin, "I am quite proud of my grapes, which are prospering beyond my expectations." "Beyond his expectations" produced tons of table grapes for Philadelphia.

The glass forcing houses are long gone, but the two massive gray walls that remain provide the powerful drama of this garden, half the size of a football field. In one corner, ivy grows from curved beds of lily-of-the-valley, forming goblet shapes of green as it climbs the wall. Wisteria tumbles over one wall. A third wall is formed by a stable of bluish fieldstone built in the 1920s, to replace one destroyed by fire. Within this U-shaped enclosure of green grass, shaggy, shoulder-high boxwoods border two intersecting paths. Under a hot sun, the boxwoods send out a pungent, crisp smell. A marble bust, fountain, and rose bed—all small and underscaled—dot the grass. As ill-conceived as they are, they do not vitiate the strength of the garden, which derives from the walls. Who ever heard of garden walls 100 feet long and 30 feet high? They should be oppressive, but they are not. Open only to the sky, the garden is a serene, contemplative contrast to the rest of Andalusia with its sparkling vistas of river, meadow, and lawns.

James Biddle, the great-great-grandson of Nicholas Biddle, lives next door in a Gothic Victorian cottage. An executive director of the National Trust for Historic Preservation during its critical formative years, he planted the Green Walk, along the open side of the Graperies.

The Green Walk is bordered on one side with juniper, holly, cherry laurel, dwarf cypress, barberry, and umbrella pine. On the other side is a perennial border of candytuft, bluebells, and alyssum with yellow, blue, and white predominating. The walk overlooks a hay meadow and tennis court, once the site of the mulberry tree fiasco.

ANDALUSIA, PO Box 158, Andalusia, PA 19020. (215) 848-1777. Owned by the Andalusia Foundation.

OPEN

House and grounds, year-round, Tuesday through Saturday, except legal holidays. By appointment only for groups of 5 or more; or for a fee of $35. Guides provided by Cliveden, a property owned by the National Trust for Historic Preservation. Tour of house takes 1 hour; visitors are then free to stroll the grounds and gardens. Admission fee.

FACILITIES

Limited access to house and grounds for people with physical disabilities; grass and gravel paths.

DIRECTIONS

Lincoln Tunnel to New Jersey Turnpike south to Exit 6 to Pennsylvania Turnpike. Take Exit 28 (US Route 1 interchange). Turn right or south on US 1 toward Philadelphia to Route 132 east (Street Road). Turn right and go 3.3 miles to a dead end, which is State Road. Turn right on State Road and go 1.7 miles. The white gates of Andalusia will be on the left.

꧁

BOWMAN'S HILL STATE WILDFLOWER PRESERVE

WASHINGTON'S CROSSING, PENNSYLVANIA

꧁ Mosquitoes are thickest in spring, which is, of course, the best time to see Bowman's Hill State Wildflower Preserve. But tolerate them. They are more than offset by the wildflower show. As the snow melts and the woods turn wet and soppy, the pale lemon sunlight of early spring filters through the bare branches of the tulip trees. Some are 100 feet tall. When the wildflowers appear, some only inches high, the scale of trees to flowers—from so big to so small—is stunning.

One by one the wildflowers fill in the sprigged carpet—crested irises, ivory-colored spring beauties, bluebells, swamp buttercups, violets, peach-colored columbines, pussy-toes, trillium, wild strawberries. Wild azaleas, lacier and paler than their domesticated counterparts, waft their delicate cinnamon perfume over the forest floor.

By May, when the tulip trees are in full leaf, the show is over and the carpet turns to its rich summertime green.

Bosky dell follows bosky dell, 100 acres in all, laced with common, rare, and endangered wildflowers, ferns, and grasses. For example, the dense blazing star (*Liatris spicata*), a commoner on midwestern prairies, is rare in Pennsylvania, found only on remnant prairies in the western part of the state.

Tanbark trails meander along Pidcock Creek. Each trail is named for a plant inhabitant, such as gentian, marshmarigold, ferns, or medicinal herbs.

Do not miss the man-made pond in the middle of the preserve, a small work of genius that won the Garden Club Founder's Award in 1950. The pond is designed so that a tiny trickle of a brook flows into it at such a slow rate that the surface of the pond moves imperceptibly. Tiny yellow-green polka dots (duckweed) barely drift among patches of green velvet, a strikingly beautiful algae with the strikingly ugly name of pond scum. The result is a changing moire pattern of textured greens.

Beneath clumps of fiddle fern, giant bullfrogs sit so immobile that they look like their ceramic parlor counterparts.

At the trail house, a bulletin board is posted with the weekly blooming of wildflowers—with color photographs, a nice touch for both wildflower neophytes and experts.

BOWMAN'S HILL STATE WILDFLOWER PRESERVE, Box 103, Washington's Crossing, PA 18977. (215) 862-2924. The preserve is administered by the Pennsylvania Historical and Museum Commission; Bowman's Hill Wildflower Preserve Association, Inc., and the Washington's Crossing Park Commission.

OPEN
Grounds and Preserve Building, Monday through Saturday, 9 A.M. to 5 P.M.; Sunday, noon to 5 P.M. No admission fee. Guided tours require advance reservation; admission fee.

FACILITIES
· Picnicking permitted nearby.
· Gift shop; Platt Bird, Nest, and Egg collection on exhibit.
· Limited access to garden for people with physical disabilities; one paved trail, rest gravel. Full access to Preserve Building.

EVENTS
· Classes in botany and horticulture, focusing on Pennsylvania's native flora, Saturday; limited to 20 people. Admission fee.
· Family Walk, every Sunday, 2 P.M.; during January and February, slide show or movie. Admission fee.

DIRECTIONS
Lincoln Tunnel to New Jersey Turnpike south to Exit 9. Take Route 1 south to I-95 west. After crossing the Delaware River, go north on Route 32 (River Road) about 6 miles to the Preserve entrance on the left.

◈

DEERFIELD

RYDAL, PENNSYLVANIA

◈ One of the most notable things about the gardens at Deerfield is the gardener himself: H. Thomas Hallowell, Jr., who zips about his 50 acres in a golf cart, pointing out this or that with enormous enthusiasm or directing the Davey tree pruners who are in residence at least one month a year.

"I don't know the name of anything," he claims as he expounds on the history of each plant that makes up his garden of vistas. (Not true—he knows the names of almost everything.)

Deerfield has never had a garden plan. "And you can't hire someone to make one for you," says Mr. Hallowell. "You look. You consider. You change. It's a very personal thing, you know."

Mr. Hallowell prizes vistas, so he makes vistas. In so doing he uses a camera, a chain saw, and a bulldozer, a machine he loves. With the camera, he frames the view, composing it into solids and voids. Then with chain saw or bulldozer, he removes the branch, tree, or hilltop that interferes with the desired mass or silhouette.

Once Mr. Hallowell razed a 15-room Tudor mansion that had come with the property, because he wanted a grander view of greensward and a prize copper beech.

Such boldness requires money and spirit, and Mr. Hallowell is richly endowed with both. The result is a "truly large American garden," as he likes to call it. There are 22 acres of lawn, studded with 100 different species of trees. Lightning rods have been installed on the more important ones. A boxwood allée runs for 700 feet, overlooking the Lower Valley Garden. Tulip trees and oaks shade a deep ravine, banked with 7,000 azaleas and dogwoods. A brook winds through Five Springs Garden, a lush glen that is host to ferns, mosses, and small blue irises. Four thousand lilies brush the hillside with a sunset of colors: apricot, peach, orange, yellow, and ivory. A managed wildflower meadow spills color all summer long: red poppies, blue chickory, daisies, asters.

But Deerfield's most popular showpiece is the maze, a half-scale replica of the maze at Hampton Court in England.

The origins of mazes are shrouded in medieval superstition, when labyrinths were planted to emulate the path of earthly travail. To gain heavenly grace, penitents would crawl on their hands and knees through the maze.

By the time the maze had reached Hampton Court—in 1690—it had fallen on more frivolous times and was simply considered garden entertainment. And so it was in America, when the fancier resorts of the nineteenth century incorporated mazes into their strolling gardens.

Like Hampton Court, the Deerfield maze was planted for fun and tomfoolery. The Hampton Court maze is yew, eight feet tall; the Deerfield maze, kept trimmed to a four-foot height, is boxwood. Boxwood is more highly prized for mazes because it is slower growing, and more densely packed than yew, and gives a cleaner edge when trimmed.

Trimming is an annual task that Mr. Hallowell often undertakes himself. It takes 32 hours to clip the ½ mile of boxwoods. He does not use a string to make a straight line. He clips by "feel," a dying art.

The Hallowells open the maze and gardens each spring. On a recent invitation, Mr. Hallowell wrote, "Forty-two years ago Dorothy and I bought this old farm. It had about 100 square feet of lawn and the rest all fields and woods. . . . We and the flowers will be glad to see you."

DEERFIELD, 980 Meetinghouse Road, Rydal, PA 19046. Mailing address: H. Thomas Hallowell, Jr., 916 The Benson East, Jenkintown, PA 19046. (215) 572-3029.

OPEN

Two days in May each year. Write Mr. Hallowell in January for the dates. No admission fee. Or you may visit anytime with the purchase of a copy of *Deerfield: An American Garden through Four Seasons*, 96 pages, with color photographs and text by Derek Fell, $35. Write Mr. Hallowell for a copy.

FACILITIES
Not accessible to people with physical disabilities.

DIRECTIONS
Lincoln Tunnel to New Jersey Turnpike south to Exit 6 to Pennsylvania Turnpike. Take Exit 27 (Willow Grove) and go south on Route 611 (Old York Road). Pass Abington Hospital (about 4 to 5 miles). At traffic light, turn left onto Susquehanna Road. Go under railroad bridge, turn left, and stay on Susquehanna Road for about ½ mile. Turn right onto Mill Road for about 200 yards, and then turn right onto Meetinghouse Road. Proceed about ⅓ mile and on the right will be a fireplug located at the entrance. Turn into the entrance and park on the grass on the right-hand side of the lane.

ELEUTHERIAN MILLS, THE HAGLEY ON THE BRANDYWINE

WILMINGTON, DELAWARE

The Brandywine River cuts a tumbling course through a steep, wooded, and rocky ravine, a site chosen by E. I. (Eleuthère Irénée) du Pont in 1802 for a black gunpowder factory.

On a bluff overlooking the workshops and mill races, Irénée, as he was known to intimates, built a modest stucco house for his beloved wife, Sophie, and their seven children. To provide food for his family and mill-workers, he sketched out a kitchen garden and ordered seeds and plants from the Jardin des Plantes in his native Paris.

The garden you see today at Eleutherian Mills is a reproduction of Irénée's original garden, reconstructed by scholars from the University of Pennsylvania and the Archeological Society of Delaware. Their findings were incorporated into a plan drawn up by landscape architect William H. Frederick in 1972.

In a wide, open meadow opposite the house, two acres of perfectly tended vegetables and flowers are planted in alternating rows—a bed of tulips, then onions; and then pansies and garlic—a configuration typical of colonial gardens.

Not so typical of colonial gardens are Irénée's "fences"—espaliered fruit trees, that march in geometric precision around the perimeter. Espalier is what makes the garden at Eleutherian Mills worth a visit.

Espalier was necessary in the Napoleonic France of Irénée's

childhood, because land was dear and family gardens small. Espalier is neither necessary nor in fashion in the United States today, and for good reason. To know how much, and where to graft, prune, and shape fruit trees requires a great deal of experience and painstaking labor.

The garden opens onto a small grassy plot dotted with cone-shaped pear trees, a form of espalier known as *en quenouille*. The other three sides of the garden are bordered with pear and apple trees, trained into flat, two-dimensional shapes. On a hillside beyond the garden, apple and pear trees grow in free-form exuberance, a pleasing contrast to the garden fence.

Without head gardener Peter Lindtner, there would be no such contrast. He has painstakingly trained the rich foliage fences, trees, and pollarded arbors into their definitive shapes. Examples of his art you will see include:

· A pleached arbor of lady apple trees, their top branches intertwined over a central graveled path.
· One border of U-shaped pear trees.
· One border of fan-shaped pear trees.
· A third border of pear trees trained into diamond shapes, called a Belgian fence.
· An apple tree fence, two feet high, the trees stunted to form a dense foliage rope that borders the garden paths, a form of espalier called a cordon.

Mr. Lindtner learned his art in his native Czechoslovakia before going "into service" for the du Ponts 16 years ago, at the gardens of Eleutherian Mills, Winterthur, and Nemours.

Weeding in tweed jacket and tam, Peter Lindtner describes the art of espalier. To shape a tree or shrub, a gardener must know when and how much to bend a branch without breaking it. Dwarf fruit tree stock is first grafted onto hardier root stock. (Pear trees have fuller blossoms, apple trees richer foliage. Dogwood, peach trees, yew, witch hazel, cotoneaster, and forsythia are also good for espaliering.) To achieve a flat shape, the tree is shorn of all branches except those on a two-dimensional plane. The remaining branches are then tied one-third the way up the desired angle for two or three weeks. Depending on growth, the branch is then cinched up closer to the desired angle. One error and the branch breaks, ruining the symmetry. Leaders are pinched back in the summer months and once again in winter. The critical period of tying and shaping a tree takes three years. Thereafter, the foliage is trimmed eight times a year. The pollarded apple fence at Eleutherian Mills has been 20 years in the making; the other fences, 8 years or more.

In Irénée's day all of this fairly placid horticultural activity was pursued against a volatile backdrop. The mill-works blew up with regularity, averaging one explosion every 14 months and a loss of three lives with each explosion. Sometimes the alarm bell of a watchman signaled the impending disaster. More often there was no warning at all. A spark would ignite the black charcoal dust, and du Ponts and workers alike would rush to wet down roofs or stockpiles of charcoal.

One such explosion in 1890 destroyed part of Irénée's house and his garden, which lay fallow until 1972 when reconstruction began.

There is a second garden on the Eleutherian Mills property, the "folly" of Louise Crowninshield, great-granddaughter of Irénée and the last du Pont to live in residence here.

When she inherited the property in the 1920s, Louise and her yachtsman husband, who sailed in the America's Cup races, converted the mill site below the house into a garden. They patterned it after the Villa d'Este, incorporating "constructed" romantic ruins, a style then in vogue.

With barrel-vaulted caves once used to boil down saltpeter as a focal point, they built terraced paths that led down to the millraces. They installed Italianate columns, marble statuary; converted a fire reservoir to a garden pond; and packed the hillside with forsythia, lilacs, azaleas, fragrant viburnums, and rhododendrons. Around the dining and seating areas on the flagstone terrace, they planted candytuft, dianthus, tulips, pansies, and English daisies.

Louise disliked the soggy winters and hot humid summers of the Brandywine valley, but she returned each spring when her folly was in bloom.

Until a decade ago, the Crowninshield garden lay under a tangle of weeds and briars. Its resurrection is in progress. By 1989 the Crowninshield garden will be open to the public who can then savor the contrast between Irénée's purposeful kitchen garden and his great-granddaughter's folly carved with a lot of money from his gunpowder mill-works.

E. I. DU PONT'S GARDEN AT ELEUTHERIAN MILLS, The Hagley on the Brandywine, PO Box 3630, Wilmington, DE 19807. (302) 658-2400.

OPEN
House and gardens, April through December, daily, 9:30 A.M. to 4:30 P.M.; January through March 31, Saturday and Sunday, 9:30 A.M. to 4:30 P.M.; weekdays, guided tour at 1:30 P.M.; closed Thanksgiving, Christmas, New Year's Day. Admission fee.

FACILITIES
· Restaurant/snack bar.
· Vending machines with snacks, beverages.
· Picnicking permitted.
· Gift shop.
· Limited access for people with physical disabilities to E. I. du Pont gardens only; gravel paths.
· Tours of the 230-acre Brandywine property include stone mills, workshops, storehouses, millrace, Blacksmith Hill, a restored workers' housing area, the Georgian-style home of E. I. du Pont, barn cooper's shop, the Du Pont Company's first office building, a museum with exhibits, working models, demonstrations.
· Guided tours of house, Monday through Friday, 1:30 P.M.

EVENTS
· Irish Festival, a weekend in April.
· Family Day, a Saturday in September.
· Crafts Fair, first weekend in November.
· Christmas at Hagley, the month of December.

DIRECTIONS
Lincoln Tunnel to New Jersey Turnpike south to Exit 6 to the Pennsylvania Turnpike. Across Delaware Memorial Bridge. Take Route 295 to Route 141 north. Follow signs to Hagley.

FAIRMOUNT PARK HORTICULTURE CENTER

PHILADELPHIA, PENNSYLVANIA

The Horticulture Center is a 22-acre parcel of Fairmount Park, at 8,900 acres, the largest urban park in the world. The Center comprises an arboretum, greenhouses, and demonstration and perennial gardens. The jewel of the park is a Japanese house and garden whose compact perfection looks right at home in this American park.

A rich feudal lord, samurai, or scholar would have lived in this sixteenth-century-style house, built in Japan of Hinoki cypress. The house was originally displayed in the garden of New York City's Museum of Modern Art in 1954 and 1955. It was then given to the city of Philadelphia. With a thousand intricately fitted pieces joined by pegs—no nails—it took over two years for Japanese workers to reassemble the three separate sections—main house, teahouse, and bathhouse.

The house and garden are inseparable. The house seems, in fact, to be an element of the garden, large scale, like the pond that takes up almost half the compound. The pond is the core of the garden, its heart shape a symbol of long life and health.

The garden provides a spiritual experience in all seasons. Spring brings the blooms of azaleas, dogwoods, and tree peonies, pink and white flowering cherry and pear trees, and white-flowering nandina, an evergreen shrub common in Japanese gardens. In summer, the garden is lush and green, with a splash of color from 25 orange, black, and white

Nishiki *koi*—carp specially bred for their brocaded patterns—that swim in the pond. Fall's colors are vibrant—red dogwoods against purple plum trees and the borrowed landscape of the yellows and oranges of trees outside the garden. In winter, the pond is frozen and still; snow ices the house eaves and drifts like miniature ocean swells across the four-foot curved top of a "snow viewing" lantern.

In this small garden, you see the landscape of Japan in miniature. A tiny rockbound island symbolizes Japan itself. On the far side of the pond, tall white pines form a backdrop to the view, a reminder of the forests of Japan. A serpentine three-step waterfall reflects the snaking path of Japanese watercourses. Even the azaleas are trimmed to suggest Japanese mountains.

It takes a bit of psychic readjustment to move the short distance from the Japanese house to the demonstration gardens. Here city dwellers glean ideas for low- and very-low-maintenance backyard plots, fruit and vegetable gardens, flowers for drying, and raised gardens for people with physical disabilities. Opposite the demonstration gardens, a border of perennials and grasses—180 feet of basic cultivars in unadventurous design—grows within the foundations of old Horticulture Hall. Built for America's centennial in 1876, the hall was destroyed in 1953 by Hurricane Hazel.

In the greenhouses, half the area is display—subtropical plants, collections of hibiscus, cacti and succulents, and seasonal flowers that change three times a year—and half is for propagation and plant care. Both areas are open to the public. And if you want to have a wedding here, you can, but plan on a long engagement. Bookings run two years in advance.

FAIRMOUNT PARK HORTICULTURE CENTER, North Horticulture Drive, Philadelphia, PA 19131. (215) 879-4062.

OPEN
- Grounds, daily, sunrise to sunset. No admission fee.
- Greenhouses, daily, 9 A.M. to 3 P.M. No admission fee.
- Japanese house, May through October, Wednesday through Sunday, 10 A.M. to 4 P.M.; after Labor Day, weekends only. Admission fee.

FACILITIES
- Picnicking permitted by permit only for groups of 10 or more.
- Japanese house not accessible to people with physical disabilities; rest of grounds is accessible.

EVENTS

- Outdoor sculpture show, August or October.
- Harvest show, end of September; community gardens enter vegetables and flowers in competition for ribbons and awards.
- Christmas tours of seven historic homes within the park, decorated for the holidays, first two weeks of December; holiday show and restaurant in the greenhouse.

DIRECTIONS

Lincoln Tunnel to New Jersey Turnpike south to Exit 7. Follow signs to Route 295 south, and continue to Route 76 north to the Walt Whitman Bridge. Cross bridge and continue on Route 76 to Montgomery Avenue exit. On Montgomery Avenue, turn left at the first triangle; at second triangle, turn left into the gate.

THE
HENRY
FOUNDATION
FOR BOTANICAL
RESEARCH

GLADWYNE, PENNSYLVANIA

❦ In the middle of this tony, horsey suburb where a private tennis court is *de rigeur* lies a well-hidden 40-acre respite—The Henry Foundation for Botanical Research. On this rolling, wooded site are many rare, and some endangered, native American plants collected half a century ago by a remarkable self-taught botanist, Mary G. Henry.

Her daughter, Josephine Henry, president and director of the Foundation, calls this naturalistic garden "a place for dedicated plants-men . . . made for the comfort of the plants." She gives visitors a detailed tour and anecdotal history, plant by plant.

The garden is dominated by a dramatic outcropping of rocks on a hill above the house where Mary Henry once lived, and which is now the Foundation headquarters. The outcropping is fringed with yuccas, gentians, and silver bells (*Halesia*). In small clearings and wooded glades below the house and bordering the drive are native species of rhododendron, styrax, fringe tree (*Chionanthus*), trillium, rare species of lily, lavender-flowered bee balm. Of particular interest are the dwarf poplar and dwarf shadbush brought back from the north bank of the Peace River in British Columbia 50 years ago.

In the late 1920s, Mary Henry set out with her car and driver to explore the continent from Florida to the Canadian Rockies. She climbed the wildest parts of mountain ranges and tramped through swamps in the South, ferreting out rare and unusual plants.

"My mother had a quick eye for color and form," reports Miss Henry. She could scan a hillside of rhododendrons and spot just the right plant—for better color, wider foliage, bigger blooms. She brought them home and planted them here, nursing each one. Sometimes she would even impoverish the soil with tennis court surfacing to make a newcomer feel more at home."

An ardent botanist herself, Miss Henry is in the process of cataloging the collection numerically, chronologically, and botanically. The task is Sisyphean, but she is always eager to set out on a botanical tour of her well-tended inheritance.

THE HENRY FOUNDATION FOR BOTANICAL RESEARCH, Henry Lane, Gladwyne, PA 19035. (215) 525-2037.

OPEN
April through October, Tuesday and Thursday, 10 A.M. to 4 P.M.; other times by appointment; groups must confirm appointments in writing. No admission fee.

EVENTS
Botanical programs, spring and fall; telephone for information.

DIRECTIONS
Lincoln Tunnel to New Jersey Turnpike south to Exit 6 to the Pennsylvania Turnpike. Get off at Exit 25 (Norristown). Veer on a gentle curve to the right; at first traffic light turn right onto Chemical Road. Pass through one traffic light and a major intersection. Get into left lane; at next traffic light, turn right onto Butler Turnpike. Go through Conshohocken (which means "bend in the river" in Lenni Lenape) and down a long hill. After crossing a bridge, turn left. At traffic light, turn left again (Mobil station will be on left) onto Route 23, Conshohocken State Road, which winds under expressway. About ½ mile beyond the traffic light is Henry Lane on the left. Turn into Henry Lane, and at a small stream, bear left onto Stony Lane to entrance on the right.

JOANNA REED'S GARDEN

MALVERN, PENNSYLVANIA

It's just a country garden." Joanna Reed smiles. Just a country garden? Yes, but a country garden of high passion, generous spirit, and experimentation.

Wisteria dangles from a porch roof. White clematis tumbles over a stone wall that embraces a comfy white frame house, circa 1804. Wooden tools hang against a patio wall. There is a garden gate that squeaks and an ancient dinner bell to summon the field hands. (There aren't any. Just Joanna.)

Below the house, a green lawn unrolls between a grape arbor, corn cribs, neat brick-edged beds of herbs and mints and unruly jumbles of coreopsis, calendulas, salvias, and yarrows. A wagon track passes a meadowful of daisies.

What looks like a free-flowing, unfettered garden is as planned and colorful as a kaleidoscope—moving pieces that produce infinite variation within a set geometric pattern. The garden rambles along stone walls—the pattern. Flowers, everchanging, provide the variation.

Over the years, Joanna has built most of the walls from fieldstones spewed up by frost heave every winter.

"When you want to build a wall, you feel entirely different about fieldstones," Joanna explains. "They become an asset."

Her first wall was dry set. "Dry set walls don't hold as well as mortared walls. Early settlers made dry walls because they were cheap. For a dry set wall, you need flat stones and great skill. The trick is a good foundation. If water seeps into the foundation through tunnels made by moles and voles, the crumbling begins. Good-bye, wall!"

Today in the garden, there are high walls, low walls, foundation walls, retaining walls. Each forms a terrace, a nook, or a backdrop for a blaze of flowers, a rock garden, a pocket of mosses.

Next to the barn, a retaining wall warms an espaliered apple tree. The elbow of the barn and the red color of the barn siding gather the southerly sun, encouraging anemones, tulips, irises, and daffodils to bloom early.

In late fall, the elbow is warm and full of color. Sedum, pale pink anemones, and late-blooming yellow chrysanthemums crowd around an old stone cistern, now a lily pond, and tumble down a rocky terrace. Beyond, the meadow blooms with pale lavender asters, five- to seven-feet tall. What Joanna calls the star of her garden, *Idesia polycarpa*, now comes to life alongside a stone wall. The tree dangles clusters of bright red fruit that last from fall until early February.

With Joanna's watchful eye on color, texture, and scale, the garden comes close to achieving the gardener's dream—a display of foliage, blooms, and seedpods that provides high interest year-round. How does she achieve such a goal?

When Joanna Reed began to garden in the early 1940s, the land was mostly open fields choked with weeds and pocked with the rotting carcasses of abandoned cars. She cleaned out aggressive, unwanted weeds and grasses, a continuing process. To native inhabitants she introduced "new" native wildings and nursery-grown domestics, plant by plant. Seeds and plants came from the Royal Horticultural Society in England, from catalogs, from friends, and arboretums. Neighbors

❧

PRECEDING PAGE: *A voluptuous tangle of color blooms from the earliest saffron crocus to showy white puffs of saltbush in late autumn.*

brought her unusual field specimens. On every sharp-eyed tramp through a meadow or wood, she might bring home a find.

The result is a garden that is an unorthodox mix of wild and nursery plants that provides showiness three seasons a year.

"Take the *Euonymus americana,* for example," Joanna cites. "It is a sturdy, awkward-looking, trashy plant. Most people would throw it out of their garden. But in October it puts out spectacular seedpods that knock your socks off. Day-Glo pink tiny pompoms. Remember the pink popcorn we used to buy at carnivals? It looks like that. It is a color you would not find in nature, but there it is! So I planted it in the woods.

"Then there is ironweed, another domestic wonder. It grows six- to seven-feet tall, with dark matte green pebblylike leaves that curl around the stem at the nodes. In fall, deep purple blossoms hang in clusters. It's often confused with Joe-Pye weed. I planted it next to the saltbush, which sends out tassels of white fluff just when the ironweed is blossoming, and also among the irises and the daylilies, which give up in late August or September. By November, the ironweed seedpods hang bright and saucy, like sable paintbrushes, a rich, lively brown."

For late winter and early spring, the dreariest time for most gardens, Joanna plants *Helleborus niger,* the Christmas rose, and *Helleborus orientalis,* the Lenten rose. Both bush out at 2½-foot height and blossom with 20 flowers or more per bush over a 6-week period.

The Christmas rose has thick, waxy, palmate leaves six inches across and fat pale green buds that change from white-suffused-with-pink to mauve.

When the Lenten rose begins to bloom, the foliage has turned brown, which Joanna cuts back, leaving clusters of blooms that range in color from purplish pink to cream and that deepen to dark maroon, often streaked or speckled. The seedpods stay green well into June.

"A long run for one plant, isn't it?" Joanna comments.

Joanna manages the woods that border the garden on two sides with the same four-season requirements. For 40 years, she has pruned, reshaped, replanted, added, and removed trees. In spring, the high-flung tulip trees spread out a pale green canopy. The tulip trees were always there. Underneath, she planted azaleas and dogwood in shades of pale pink and salmon. Violets poke out from pincushions of moss. In clearing underbrush, she left exposed a cedar tree skeleton. Its antler-shaped limbs make a fine sculpture, black against green fern fronds in summer; black against snow in winter.

In autumn, the tulip trees, now a wall of brilliant yellow, are the backdrop for sweet gums, their star-shaped leaves sparkling like garnets. The sweet pepperbush that has slumbered in a dull green all summer long blossoms into a shower of gold. The leaves are high-gloss yellow, the berries a duller, burnished Florentine gold, hanging in pendulous clusters from olive green stems.

Against the white stucco and clapboard house, a crab apple transforms itself seasonally. In spring it is a puff of white and pink, lustrous green in summer. In winter when its ebony branches are glazed with ice, thousands of winter berries dot the tree like cinnamon red-hots.

Joanna began gardening reluctantly, growing vegetables under the direction of her father-in-law during World War II. She gradually switched to flowers. Then, she says, "Barnes Arboretum and Elizabeth Farley changed my life. I trained under her. She was wonderful! I took botany, ecology, and plant history for three years. Free! No degrees. We collected and experimented. I gardened by myself four days a week when I was lucky enough to get the time. I had five children."

That was 40 years ago. Now she still gardens four days a week, mostly by herself, all 37 acres, 4 of them intensively.

"I enjoy the whole thing or I wouldn't do it. I never get it all done. I do it for my pleasure. And I like to share that pleasure. When I don't get pleasure, I won't do it any more."

About 2,000 visitors "drop in" each year to share the pleasure.

And when it gets too cold or dark to work outside, she drags her garden inside. She is an expert needlewoman. "Gardening with wool," she calls it. Her house is full of pillows, window seat cushions, and draperies she has embroidered. And she gives lectures. And orders seeds. And reads about gardening. And waits for spring.

JOANNA REED'S GARDEN, Longview Farm, PO Box 76, RD 1, Malvern, PA 19355. (215) 827-7614.

OPEN
April through October, Friday, noon to dusk. Do not call in advance, just go; except groups, which are by appointment. Admission fee for groups only.

FACILITIES
· Picnicking permitted.
· Partially accessible to wheelchairs.

DIRECTIONS

Lincoln Tunnel to New Jersey Turnpike south to Exit 6 to the Pennsylvania Turnpike to Exit 24 (Valley Forge). Go south on Route 202 toward West Chester for about 9 miles. Exit at Route 401 west, and go through two traffic lights. At top of steep hill, turn onto Valley Hill Road (unmarked). Go ⅛ mile and take the left fork at the stop sign. Continue straight down a short hill. Joanna Reed's is last house on left before road crosses a bridge. Park in meadow on right side of road.

JOHN BARTRAM'S GARDEN

PHILADELPHIA, PENNSYLVANIA

A glorious garden this is not, but for the botanical historian a visit is a must. Its 10 acres are all that remain of America's oldest surviving botanical garden.

As royal botanist to King George III, John Bartram pushed west to the Ohio River and as far south as Georgia to find new plant specimens. He brought them home in the watertight bladders of oxen, to propagate on the banks of the Schuylkill River.

Most of his discovered species grow in the Bartram garden today, including his most famous, the Franklin tree (*Franklinia alatamaha*), found on the banks of the Alatamaha River in Florida. Now extinct in the wild, the tree is a decorative garden favorite because its waxy white camellialike blossoms appear so late in the year, usually August or September.

Below the house and barn on land stretching down to the river are prickly ash (the toothache tree, valued for the painkilling propensities of its bark); the bald cypress, which Bartram discovered in Delaware; the Fraser magnolia, which he brought home from Cherokee country, now the Great Smoky National Park; and the cucumber magnolia, found on the shores of Lake Ontario when he accompanied a peace mission to the Iroquois Nations in upstate New York. A pawpaw tree is in the garden. Bartram once sent its fruit and flower to England preserved in a bottle of rum.

Over a 40-year period, this indefatigable Quaker sent over 200 plant species "home" to England, including the mountain laurel, which quickly became a staple in the English landscape.

Bartram himself was a messy farmer. His plants were never arranged in orderly fashion, rare specimens often concealed by weeds and briars. So it is today. The kitchen and formal flower gardens are scruffy and studded with weeds. While a weed-choked garden may be historically correct, the memory of America's premier botanist would be better served by better maintenance.

JOHN BARTRAM'S GARDEN, 54th Street and Lindbergh Boulevard, Philadelphia, PA 19143. (215) 729-5281. Owned by city of Philadelphia; maintained by Fairmount Park Commission. The John Bartram Association administers programs and owns period furnishings in the house.

OPEN
- Garden, daily, dawn to dusk. No admission fee.
- House, May 1 through October 31, Wednesday through Sunday, 12 noon to 4 P.M.; November through April, Wednesday through Friday, 12 noon to 4 P.M. Admission fee.

FACILITIES
- Box lunches for 10–50 persons may be ordered 10 days in advance.
- Picnicking permitted.
- Gift shop.
- Garden accessible to wheelchairs, but house is not.

EVENTS
- Group house and garden tours with slide show for adults, with advance reservations, Tuesday through Friday, 10 A.M. to 4 P.M. Admission fee.
- Drop-in house tour, Tuesday through Friday, 10 A.M. to 4 P.M. Admission fee.
- Tea and house tour (5–15 people), Tuesday through Friday afternoons; adults only. Advance reservations required. Admission fee.

DIRECTIONS
Lincoln Tunnel to New Jersey Turnpike south to Exit 4. Go south on I-295 to Route 76 west. Cross the Walt Whitman Bridge and go to Passyhunk Avenue. Turn west on Passyhunk to Lindbergh Boulevard. Turn north on Lindbergh. Garden entrance is on the right just before 54th Street.

LONGWOOD GARDENS

In your first half hour at Longwood, you will want to toast
Pierre S. du Pont—as a man who passionately loved trees, gardens,
and water spectacles; and for his directive that after his death
Longwood be maintained as a public garden of "beauty and entertainment."

Because of this directive, implemented with a huge endowment,
Longwood today is the premiere horticultural display garden on the
Eastern seaboard, unparalleled in floral showmanship.

Every aspect is blue ribbon. In the conservatories hardly a spent
flower needs dead-heading. Not a twig of topiary straggles out of place.
In the water gardens, all 1,500 water jets work. Meticulously groomed
gardens roll out, one after another, across 350 acres: a grand allée in the
French tradition, very American backyard flower beds, English cottage

gardens, a pastoral hunting park, a Victorian grotto, peony, wisteria, and rose gardens, and wildflower meadows.

The Longwood staff is as dedicated to tending visitors as it is plants. Horticultural interns cheerfully answer questions as they trim and clip or groom the black soil with rakes so tiny they look like combs.

Benches are there when benches are needed. In a heavy rain, giant green and white umbrellas are loaned, courtesy of the management. In the sunny, plant-filled restaurant, the menu is inventive. (It includes four mushroom dishes, Kennett Square being the mushroom capital of the world.)

Where to begin a delicious day of exploration? Where Pierre du Pont began, with his first love, the water gardens.

Six-year-old Pierre was fascinated by the water displays at the 1876 Philadelphia Centennial and by Frederick Olmsted's watercourses at Chicago's 1893 Columbian Exposition. Like most privileged young men of his day, Pierre toured Europe with his family after graduating from MIT. The European water spectacles delighted him—the broad, flat reflecting canals of Versailles, the water staircase at Villa d'Este, the channels and fountains of the Villa Gori in Siena.

These memories, long tucked away, emerged when he acquired Longwood at the age of 40. In 1915, with virtually unlimited funds, du Pont began to develop his beloved water gardens.

The Main Fountain Garden is a sunken five-acre expanse of broad lawns, moats, canals, and fountains. Some jets are tiny silver threads of water; others, geysers that surge 130 feet into the air.

During five-minute water shows, the jets thunder skyward in single spouts, then change into crossing arcs, finally melting into fan-shaped sheets of fine water spray that glint with rainbows.

In this sunken garden, water spouts from the mouths of carved limestone nymphs, frogs, fish, and mythical creatures into pools and huge limestone basins. The water fractures the surface into thousands of dancing light prisms. By contrast, the moat that circles the island of boxwood in the center of the garden is either a glassy mirror or a ruffled ring of water, depending on the breeze. Double rows of Norway maples, trimmed to box shapes, make a cool, shady promenade around these glittering water gardens on a hot day.

On summer evenings the garden is transformed into a Festival of

࿔

PRECEDING PAGE: *Three times daily during the summer, 200 water jets thunder skyward in arcs, fans, and geysers in the Main Fountain Garden.*

Fountains, a computerized extravaganza of music, water, and rainbow-colored lights. With 17,300,000 possible combinations in a 30-minute show, the fountains outsparkle their French counterpart, the *Son et Lumière* at Versailles.

The Italian Water Garden is an intimate, leafy refuge in sharp contrast to the rest of Longwood's flamboyance. This gray, green, and watery world is on two levels, surrounded by hemlocks and lindens. A limestone balustraded terrace overlooks blue-tiled pools, orderly rectangles of grass, pearly gray stone walls, and fountains banked with ivy.

The sound of water soothes. Single strands of water arc across the blue pools. Water from the fountains drips into stone troughs along two sides of the garden. Silver ribbons of water sluice down a water staircase, churning into white water in a pool at the bottom.

Pierre's third water fancy is an Open Air Theatre, conceived as were all his gardens for pleasure and entertainment. Over the years Pierre's June garden parties became legendary social events. A theatrical staged in an outdoor theater was always a highlight. Imagine the astonishment of guests on a June night in 1916 when the theatrical ended in a floodlit shower of water. Damsels in diaphanous white slowly waltzed to a stop. Rings of water shot up around the dancers as a water screen rose behind them.

Today the water is used as a curtain for the musicales held in the Open Air Theatre. A short water display follows each performance.

After the water gardens, the conservatories are Longwood's most sumptuous spectacle—great bell jars spilling forth warmth, moist earth smells, perfume, and flowers.

There are seven conservatories in all, three-and-a-half acres under glass. But the main floral exhibitions are staged in the Orangerie, a 1920s crystal palace with 25-foot arched windows, and in the modern East Conservatory, capped by an oval dome with diamond-shaped panels.

Masses of flowers border lawns of baby-fine grass. Flowers tumble in cascades down ivied pillars, hang from baskets, and are fashioned into topiary trees and set out in tubs. Most dramatically, they hang from globes five feet in diameter. In spring the globes are covered with thousands of marguerite daisies and forget-me-nots; in summer, with pink geraniums; and in fall with mums. For the Christmas show, the globes spangle with a display of poinsettias in a spectrum of hot pink, red, salmon, and cream shot with pale pink or pale green.

This wizardry with flowers is labor intensive. For the mum show, the wizardry begins when Longwood propagates thousands of seedlings. The seedlings are then transplanted into wire baskets and trained along wire armatures. As plants mature, they are pinched for fewer, fuller blooms and are sheared weekly until buds start to form. Nine wire armatures planted with mums are finally connected to make each globe.

Surprisingly, only twice a year is anything planned on paper for the main conservatories. Rather, flower beds are replenished from a steady supply of fresh blooms in the production greenhouses.

The head gardener and chief designer stroll through the conservatories noting what flowers are past prime and what is coming into peak in the greenhouse.

"It's like cooking," explains Landon Scarlett, planning and design manager. "First you look and see what's in the refrigerator. Then you plan the menu. Where to fill in color. What scale. What texture. . . . Accidents happen. Sometimes seeds don't germinate. Sometimes plants don't bloom when they're supposed to."

The more-or-less permanent backdrop of greenery for the hothouse flowers includes Australian tree fern, acacia trees, rhododendrons, creeping fig on the pillars, and, new in 1987, hymenosporum, an evergreen native of Australia that grows to 50 feet.

The Orangerie and East Conservatory interconnect with five other conservatories that house, among other things, a Desert House, a Palm House, a collection of insect-devouring plants, and 6,000 species of orchids in several greenhouses, each with different temperatures and humidity levels. Each week the peak blooms are removed from the greenhouses and placed in an orchid showroom.

In the East Conservatory children can wander through a maze of ivy in the Children's Garden. In the vegetable garden, a ball of parsley hangs from the ceiling, over raised beds of lettuce, red-stemmed rhubarb, and espaliered nectarine trees and grapevines.

Visitors can stroll through the backstage production greenhouses where students, interns, and gardeners undertake propagation and plant maintenance chores.

Outdoors there are 18 separate garden areas to explore, set among an arboretum of 200-year-old trees, all buffered from the outside world by an additional 650 acres of forest and managed meadows.

Because Pierre du Pont distrusted landscape architects, he laid out his own gardens. "Like Wanamaker's," as he was fond of explaining, "department after department." Thus Longwood's specialty gardens march along the paths, man-made ravines, and waterfalls, with no apparent plan.

The Flower Garden Walk is stocked with Pierre du Pont's

old-fashioned favorites: roses, hollyhocks, lilacs, tulips, irises, peonies, and snapdragons. Two beds that run for 600 feet along either side of a brick path are a bountiful mix of formal and informal plantings.

For two weeks each June, the Rose Arbor is smothered with large single-petaled, cherry red roses, the American Pillar climber. The arbor rings a sunken circular terrace of concrete imbedded with white pebbles, dazzling in the sun against green clipped lawns.

The Hillside Garden tumbles its way downhill with a chime tower as a backdrop. Korean azaleas, white candytuft, bluebells, and yellow alyssum are layered into rocky shelves that descend to a pond.

In the Topiary Garden, 60 yew trees, trimmed into cone shapes, bells, drums, and cylinders, march in parade formation down a bright green turf.

For the family gardener, an Idea Garden demonstrates different methods of propagation, irrigation, and mulching in small plots of fruits, vegetables, and ground covers.

There is a Heather and Heath Garden, a Peony and Wisteria Garden, and a lake with a Grecian temple.

For this bountiful state of horticultural affairs, we have to thank the original du Pont millions, astronomically increased by Pierre after he purchased controlling stock in the company in 1915. That same year, at age 45, this supposedly confirmed bachelor married his cousin Alice Belin and began the serious development of Longwood.

Even though du Pont enlarged the original three-story brick farmhouse, built in 1730 by Quaker owner George Peirce, it remained a modest house for one of the world's wealthiest men. In an era when millionaires lavished fortunes on opulent mansions with grand ballrooms, Pierre spent his on gardens, where he entertained sumptuously.

When he died at the age of 84, he had poured $25 million into Longwood and left it a stock portfolio now valued at $200 million.

The present stewards of Longwood pay close attention to Pierre's directive to provide public gardens for beauty and entertainment. Long-range plans are developed and approved by an advisory landscape committee that includes du Pont family members, trustees, staff, and guest professionals. A garden-by-committee is rare enough. One that works is rarer still. The result is the unmatched horticultural display at Longwood where, as at Wanamaker's, the customer is always right.

LONGWOOD GARDENS, PO Box 501, Route 1, Kennett Square, PA 19348-0501. (215) 388-6741.

OPEN
- Gardens, daily, 9 A.M. to 6 P.M.; November through March, 9 A.M. to 5 P.M. Admission fee.
- Conservatories and shops, daily, 10 A.M. to 5 P.M. or later during special events and holiday displays.
- Peirce/du Pont House, daily, April through December, 11 A.M. to 3 P.M. April and May weekends, 11 A.M. to 4 P.M. Admission fee.

FACILITIES
- Restaurant and cafeteria; reservations required for restaurant, (215) 388-6771.
- Picnicking permitted.
- Gift shop.
- Gardens, conservatories, and shops accessible to people with physical disabilities.

EVENTS
- Welcome Spring, indoor spring flower display, late January through April.
- 350 Acres of Spring, outdoors, April, May.
- Autumn Color, September, October.
- Indoor and outdoor Chrysanthemum Festival, November.
- Indoor Christmas display of poinsettias; outdoor trees lighted.
- Festival of Fountains, a half-hour display of illuminated fountains, mid-June through August; Tuesday, Thursday, Saturday at 9:15 P.M.
- Daily water shows in summer at noon, 2 P.M., and 4 P.M.
- Fireworks, one Friday evening in July, August, and September; dates announced March 1. Tickets must be purchased in advance by mail.
- Band concerts, ballet, musicals in Open Air Theatre, mid-June through August on weekends, some afternoons, but mostly evening performances. No admission fee.
- Organ and chorale concerts, fall through spring, mostly Sundays and holidays; all seating unreserved, 350 capacity. No admission fee.
- Children's programs of parades, music, games, puppet shows, drama, year-round, mostly weekends. Reservations (mail only) for some events.
    (For information on all the above, send a self-addressed business-size envelope to Schedule, Longwood Gardens, PO Box 501, Kennett Square, PA 19348.)
- Continuing education programs in gardening, horticulture, and historical topics; March through June, September through December. For a continuing education brochure, call (215) 388-6741,

144

extension 516, 8 A.M. to 11:30 A.M. and 12:30 P.M. to 4 P.M. weekdays.

- Professional training programs: Professional Gardener Training Program (2 years); International Horticultural Trainee Program (1 year); Graduate Program in Public Horticultural Administration offered in conjunction with the University of Delaware (2 years); variable length horticultural internships.

DIRECTIONS
Lincoln Tunnel to New Jersey Turnpike south to Exit 2, Route 322 west, across Commodore Barry Bridge into Pennsylvania. Continue on Route 322 west—which becomes I-95 south for about a mile or so until it branches off again, toward West Chester. At intersection with Route 1, turn left onto Route 1 south and continue for 8 miles. Entrance ramp leads from Route 1 to Longwood gates.

MEADOWBROOK
FARM

MEADOWBROOK, PENNSYLVANIA

~& Meadowbrook Farm is a splashy, colorful mix of commercial greenhouse, nursery, garden shop, and public display garden. It is also 12 separate, private gardens created by J. Liddon Pennock, Jr., owner of Meadowbrook. These small gardens, on four levels behind Mr. Pennock's stone house, are theatrical stage settings, designed as extensions to the house. Each is formal, sophisticated, and groomed to perfection. Some are to be looked at; others to be sat in. Any one would make an elegant town house garden.

They overflow with pink, white, and blue flowers, greenery walls, statuary, topiaries, epergnes, and stone containers filled with boxwood and ivy. There are four pools, many garden gates, and seven gazebos, real and faux. Mr. Pennock is not above faux anything. One Grecian temple is constructed of pine beams, plaster, and Styrofoam lintels.

The same plants—ivy, begonias, impatiens, pansies—are used over and over again, providing a strong visual link that carries from garden to garden.

Although Mr. Pennock repeats the use of these garden stalwarts, the artistry of the gardens stems from the way he arranges them. He plants impatiens and begonias in ovals and circles, alternating them with rings of baby-fine grass and 50 varieties of ivy. The ivy is fashioned into swags, balls, cascades, and espaliered along stair risers. Trees and shrubs are trimmed, bent, bedecked, arranged, and rearranged to achieve a certain "look" that varies from season to season.

One Easter, Mr. Pennock pruned a pair of 20-foot hollies until they looked like prickly green poles. He hung them with Easter eggs. When Easter was over, he continued to prune them. Today they stand, two spearlike sentries, at the top of a short staircase.

Such decisive pruning requires a fearlessly directive gardener, which Mr. Pennock is. "I want no one's view to wander," he states. "I *want* it to go in one direction. So I block a view, or give the eye only one place to look. Then I reveal little mysteries, little surprises." This he does by his placement of hedges, walks, statuary, and many, many movable pots.

Mr. Pennock's directive gardening style is immediately apparent on a tour that begins at Eagle Garden, so named for a large eagle statue that blocks the view down a narrow steep hill, diverting it along a grassy esplanade with glimpses of fountains and pools that reflect, drip, and splash.

The Eagle Garden is bordered with masses of purple and pink begonias, white impatiens, and ivy. Camellias and a bull bay magnolia are espaliered against the house. They survive Pennsylvania winters, according to Mr. Pennock, because the U-shape of the house creates a pocket-sized microclimate, collecting southerly sun and blocking the prevailing winter northerlies.

Next comes the Herb Garden, for looking not eating. Beds of crinkly Black-Seeded Simpson lettuce are bordered with parsley and yellow and red ornamental peppers. Rosemary topiaries in huge terra-cotta pots are set about on red-brick paving, as are nineteenth-century funerary chairs. These diminutive wrought-iron chairs, designed at ¾ scale to fit around a gravesite, give the garden an Alice-in-Wonderland quality. When a large man—and Mr. Pennock is not small—sits in one of the chairs, the garden instantly grows smaller, or the man bigger.

Directly below the Eagle Garden is a narrow grassy path flanked with hedges of blue dwarf sawara cypress, trimmed so that they resemble mini-Christmas trees about one foot high. Behind them, standing with military precision, is a row of standard hardy orange trees, "trimmed and trimmed and trimmed for 25 years." By now, they are dense giant green globes dotted with yellow-orange fruit on stalks 15 feet high.

Twelve steps down is the Round Garden, dominated by circles of pink begonias and white impatiens, each separated by circlets of baby-fine grass. These concentric circles of pink, white, and green ring a circular fountain. Even the rotating jet throws out a circlet of water.

Down yet another level is a small aquamarine swimming pool

tucked into a terrace of green and white. Evergreen topiaries in stone epergnes drip with white impatiens. Branches of a blue Atlas cedar hang over the pale blue-green rectangle of water. From each corner, jets send bisecting arcs of water over the pool.

The theatricality of these pocket-sized gardens reflects Mr. Pennock's passion: decorating beautiful environments for important events—museum openings, debutant parties, and balls for such clients as the Mellons, the du Ponts, and the Richard Nixons. He "did" Tricia Nixon's wedding; decorated the White House for Christmas and for an *intime* Sunday supper for Prince Charles and Princess Anne.

What do you do after you "do" the White House? Mr. Pennock's fantasy is a gangster funeral, an unlikely fantasy for a birthright Quaker, which he is. And although he refers to himself as "just a pot plant grower," he is also a member of the Social Register, a trustee of the Philadelphia Symphony, and president of Philadelphia's prestigious Academy of Music.

Partially retired, he keeps a Quakerly merchant's eye on the garden shop, the greenhouse, and the nurseries just down the hill from his house.

The garden shop specializes in potted plants, statuary, pottery, and topiary whimsies. You can buy an ivy turtle, an ivy teddy bear, an ivy hanging angel, and even a tennis racket made of ivy, spagnum moss, and fishing line.

MEADOWBROOK FARM, GREENHOUSE & NURSERY, 1633 Washington Lane, Meadowbrook, PA 19046. (215) 887-5900.

OPEN
- Shop and greenhouse, daily, except Sunday and holidays, 10 A.M. to 5 P.M.
- Private gardens, April through June, only to groups of 15 to 25, by appointment. No admission fee.

FACILITIES
- Plant and gift shop.
- Not accessible to people with physical disabilities.

DIRECTIONS
Lincoln Tunnel to New Jersey Turnpike south to Exit 6 to Pennsylvania Turnpike, to Exit 27 (Willow Grove Interchange). Go south on Route 263 to Route 63 (Old York Road). Turn right (east) onto Welsh Road to Washington Lane. Meadowbrook Farm is at junction of Meadowbrook Road and Washington Lane.

MORRIS
ARBORETUM OF
THE UNIVERSITY OF
PENNSYLVANIA

PHILADELPHIA, PENNSYLVANIA

֍ Morris Arboretum is a quintessential Victorian landscape of rolling hills, a groomed great park, woodsy glens, rose and Japanese rock gardens, looped by the Wissahickon Creek. The original owners, a rich Quaker brother and sister, John and Lydia Morris, scoured the world for plants for their beloved country seat, Compton.

Compton, the house, is long gone, but the grounds remain with 166 acres of Victorian delights: a fernery, a Temple of Love on Swan Pond, a secret grotto, and pergolas overlooking a formal walled rose garden.

Morris laid out the first 26 acres around Compton with the help of an Americanized English landscape architect, Charles Miller.

In the prevailing fashion of the late nineteenth century, he and Morris dotted lawns with one-of-a-kind specimen trees. They also clustered trees in the landscape traditions of Sir Humphrey Repton and Andrew Downing.

It is this clustering, a kind of clump school of landscape architecture, added to through the years, that gives high interest to the arboretum. Here are some examples of such massing:

- A big patch of cow parsnips grows in a small hollow. A relative of Queen-Anne's-lace, the parsnip sends out its blossoms on beet red stalks 12 feet high. The blossoms measure three feet across. Clustered together, these giant lace umbrellas are a noble sight. They make a haven for bees who drum out a steady hum of honey gathering in early summer.
- Twelve dawn redwoods are planted in a grove beside Wissahickon Creek, rather than strung out, one tree at a time, along the stream.
- Near the redwoods, a four-foot-high brass frog sits in another clump, this one a huge circle of chartreuse-colored dwarf bamboo shoots.
- On a hillside, 16 cone-shaped cedars are grouped together. They range in height from 6 to 60 feet. As a breeze moves across them, the foliage billows in rolling waves, a mesmerizing movement that would not be possible had the cedars been planted singly.

In his rock garden, Morris and his Japanese landscape gardener grouped the rocks with great care. Some are upended; some stacked horizontally; some arranged in asymmetrical groupings. The placements clearly were influenced by Morris's travels to the Orient.

While Morris clustered plantings to dramatize the pastoral scene, today they are clustered for scientific reasons. Trees planted in orchards benefit from the introduction of fresh genetic stock through pollination, a process called "out-breeding." Such out-breeding has long been common in improving strains of corn, wheat, oats, and other commercial crops, but with trees it is in its infancy.

Two Victorian showpieces of the arboretum are the newly restored Fernery, a steamy indoor grotto housing 500 varieties of tropical ferns, and the formal parterred rose garden with balustrades and fountains. "Behind every rose garden," says arboretum director Bill Klein, "is a lot of muscle, money, and manure." The sunken rose garden, laid out in traditional beds, has sensitive design details. Bunches of purple alyssum tumble through cracks of a dry set stone wall. The risers of semicircular

❧

PRECEDING PAGE: *The Marion Rivinus Rose Garden.*

stairs are planted with the palest of green succulents. A wisteria allée, pruned to a 10-foot height, flanks one side of the rose garden.

The flourishing state of affairs at Morris Arboretum—increased membership, funds, and professional staff—is the result of a partnership between board chairman F. Otto Haas (of Rohm & Haas, manufacturers of chemicals) and Bill Klein, hired by Haas as the arboretum's first full-time director. Together they reinvigorated the arboretum as a research and teaching facility for the university's landscape design and horticultural departments, concentrating on the propagation of plant species that thrive in urban settings.

To that end, Paul Meyer, curator and director of horticulture, went to Korea in 1979, 1981, and 1984. On the shores of the Yellow Sea between China and Korea, he found a golden-rain tree (*Koelreuteria paniculata*) that thrived despite severe winters, hot summers, salt spray, and impoverished sandy soil. Would this tree make a good city dweller? He brought back seedlings to propagate and investigate. *Koelreuteria paniculata* puts out rich yellow panicles in late June or early July, which would make the tree a colorful follow-up to the Bradford pear, a currently popular city tree, whose white blossoms have gone to leaf by late April. (A golden-rain tree planted long ago can be seen along the path just inside the visitors' entrance.)

In searching for the answer, two staff researchers are subjecting the Korean transplants, now 10 feet tall, to applications of salt spray. If by 1990 these introductions prove themselves, the arboretum will provide propagation materials to other botanic gardens and nurseries.

MORRIS ARBORETUM OF THE UNIVERSITY OF PENNSYLVANIA, 9414 Meadowbrook Avenue, Philadelphia, PA 19118. (215) 247-5777. Visitor information, (215) 242-3399.

OPEN
Daily, April through October, 10 A.M. to 5 P.M.; Thursday evenings in June, July, August, until 8 P.M. November through March, daily, 10 A.M. to 4 P.M. Closed Christmas and New Year's Day. Tours, Saturday and Sunday, 2 P.M.; other times by reservation only. Admission fee.

FACILITIES
· Picnicking permitted.
· Partially accessible to people with physical disabilities.

EVENTS
Seminars and classes on botany, landscape design, horticulture, and natural history. Admission fee. Call the education department, (215) 247-5777 for information.

DIRECTIONS
Lincoln Tunnel to New Jersey Turnpike south to Exit 6 to Pennsylvania Turnpike, to Exit 25 (Norristown). Turn south on Germantown Avenue, and go to junction with Northwestern Avenue. Visitors' entrance is on Hillcrest Avenue, between Germantown and Stenton avenues.

NEMOURS
MANSION AND
GARDENS

WILMINGTON, DELAWARE

⁊꙰ Nemours is about grandeur: a 102-room mansion flanked by formal gardens and an extraordinary axis of gardens and monuments that extends in a straight line from the front door to a Temple of Love a third of a mile away. Elements reminiscent of Versailles—pools, fountains, classically shaped urns, parterres, flamboyant sculpture— ornament the length of the axis.

Alfred I. duPont built Nemours in 1909 to 1910 for all the du Ponts to envy. The estimated cost was $2 million. John Carrère and Thomas Hastings, architects of the New York Public Library, designed the mansion and gardens as a unit. But the central axis was created in stages over the next 25 years, at the same time as duPont's cousins Pierre and Henry were developing Longwood and Winterthur. The gardens are maintained today to look as they did at the time of duPont's death in 1935.

The central axis is interrupted at the halfway point by a massive limestone colonnade, a memorial to Alfred duPont's forebears who came from Nemours, France. Three distinct sections lead to the colonnade. First, tall Japanese cedars, pink-flowering horse chestnuts, and pin oaks border a series of sloping grass "landings" 20 feet deep, separated by broad stone steps. On either side of the stone steps is a monumental urn planted with tulips, begonias, or chrysanthemums in season.

In the second section, a reflecting pool, which takes up an entire acre, is chaperoned by marble statues representing the four seasons. When the 157 water jets are turned off, the still surface of the pool reflects the grass landings and trees.

An intricate maze garden of hemlock and holly hedges comes next. The maze was built on a slight incline so that the pattern could be seen from the mansion.

Beyond the colonnade, an extravaganza of dazzling marble heralds a sunken garden. A marble wall and the pool at its base are crowded with sculptured cherubs, mythical beasts, and classical heads, all spouting water. A trio of basins juts out from the wall, overflowing with water. Fountains bubble and spurt. On either side of this glorious excess, twin curved staircases descend to the garden.

The sunken garden is quiet by comparison. Parterres of box and begonias are lined by shrub borders. More sculptured heads—verdigris this time—spout water from niches on each side.

Across a small, still pond and up a grassy rise, the long progression of gardens ends at the Temple of Love and its statue of Diana the Huntress.

Vastly different in scale are the two gardens at the side of the mansion. On an adjoining terrace, precision-edged white gravel paths surround intricate French parterres of boxwood, ageratum, and begonias. The English-style garden nearby, a jumble of annual and perennial standards (not an exotic variety among them), is outstanding mainly for the combined length of its four borders—800 feet in all.

Off to one side of the central axis, a rock garden is sparsely planted with dwarf conifers, species tulips, and narcissus—and peopled with, of all things, Czechoslovakian figurines made of painted plaster.

A visit to Nemours starts with a 90-minute tour of the mansion, including orange juice elegantly served from a silver tray on the back

❦

PRECEDING PAGE: *From the top of the colonnade, the view stretches across the maze garden and reflecting pool to the mansion.*

terrace. The tour is full of detailed information, splendid antiques, and works of art and includes the "downstairs" of the grand life—kitchen, pantry, bathroom, ice-making plant used before the days of freon, and an air-conditioned six-car, one-boat garage.

NEMOURS MANSION AND GARDENS, Rockland Road, PO Box 109, Wilmington, DE 19899. (302) 651-6912.

OPEN
May through November, Tuesday through Saturday, tours at 9 A.M., 11 A.M., 1 P.M., 3 P.M.; Sunday, 11 A.M., 1 P.M., 3 P.M. Reservations recommended for individuals and required for groups. Visitors must be over 16. Reservations office open Monday through Friday, 8:30 A.M. to 4:30 P.M. Admission fee includes gardens, which visitors are free to explore after the tour of the mansion.

FACILITIES
Mansion not accessible to people with physical disabilities; gardens have limited accessibility.

DIRECTIONS
Lincoln Tunnel to New Jersey Turnpike south to the end, to Delaware Memorial Bridge, to Route I-95 north (toward Wilmington). Take Exit 8 north onto Route 202 (Concord Pike). Go to second traffic light, and turn left onto Route 141. Go to second traffic light, and turn left onto Rockland Road. Nemours is on the right.

THE
SCOTT ARBORETUM
OF SWARTHMORE
COLLEGE

The Scott Arboretum is a giant demonstration garden. Located on 110 acres of the Swarthmore College campus, it grandly fulfills its purpose as a place where amateur gardeners can see the best and easiest plants to grow in the Delaware Valley. Horticultural delights are everywhere, along campus roadways and paths, in the middle of lawns, in the lee of contemporary and neo-Gothic buildings—beauty and botany by osmosis.

The Arboretum is an intriguing landscape of botanical bits and pieces—plant collections and plant combinations. "Designed" gardens are few, but these are choice: the Sue Schmidt Garden in the Cherry Border and the Scott Offices' garden.

Plantings in collections make it easier to compare varieties of a single genus, especially since the Arboretum gets highest honors for its labeling. Small collections of yellow winter hazels (*Corylopsis*), viburnums, lilacs, quinces, and catalpas grow in casual groupings. Stretched along a walk, 20 varieties of butterfly bush (*Buddleia*) flutter with the butterflies that give the shrub its name. Dozens of tree peonies fill a triangle created by intersecting campus paths. Larger collections— hollies, rhododendrons, pines, and shade trees—ring the Arboretum's perimeter.

The combination plantings—perennials, dwarf conifers, a fragrance garden, shrubs—instruct as well as please, giving gardeners ideas to try at home. Along the top of a dry stone wall, euphorbia, thyme, lavender, helianthemum, and *Sedum Sieboldii* bake in the sun.

Nearby, an alluring Summer Border of flowering shrubs surrounds half the Old Library building. Some shrubs are as small as hassocks, others tall as street lamps. Most are rarely seen in a suburban backyard. Here are pink-panicled tamarisk, hibiscus, gold flower, white-plumed false spirea, 10 species of hydrangea, and 4 species of clethra. The violet spires of a chaste tree (*Vitex Agnus-castus*) and an orchid-flowered crape myrtle mix royally with purple smokebush. Crimson trumpet vine heralds a doorway, and mock orange suffuses the air with intense perfume.

A garden of ornamental plants that thrive in the Delaware Valley was the dream of Arthur Hoyt Scott, Swarthmore '95 and son of a founder of the Scott Paper Company. Scott was an avid gardener, frustrated at the lack of arboretums in the region and averse to traveling as far as Rochester to see examples of the lilacs he wanted to collect. His death in 1927 cut short his dream of creating an arboretum. Two years later, his family established the Scott Arboretum in his memory.

When John Wister became the Arboretum's first director in 1931, only an allée of swamp white oaks and a few large oaks and hemlocks dotted the campus. The rest was reclaimed farmland. Starting at the southwest end of the Arboretum, Wister planted in botanical sequence counterclockwise around the campus, from the simplest plants—ginko, yew, and pine families—to the most complex, the *Compositae*.

Something is in bloom nine months of the year in front of an eccentric-looking double-domed building that houses the Scott Offices, once the observatory of the college's first astronomer. In this high-impact perennial garden, flowers begin early in March with the yellows of winter aconite and a tiny five-inch daffodil, *Narcissus asturiensis*. The Japanese roof iris (*Iris tectorum* 'Alba'), pure white with delicately crinkled falls (the three hanging petals of an iris), blooms in late spring. The name, "iris of the roofs," means the plant will grow under dry conditions; it doesn't grow on roofs in most areas but will thrive and spread on the ground. In summer, white heather and 'Hidcote' lavender sprawl onto the flagstone path that moves through the garden's two levels. By November, you can still find white Japanese anemones and Nippon daisies in a protected corner. A dry stone wall, hollies, and rhododendrons serve as backbone for the garden, which is a fine introduction to the Arboretum.

Across from the Scott Offices, the Cherry Border—35 varieties of flowering cherries—edges three sides of a long grass rectangle, forming a deep, serene pocket. A swing made from a slab of wood hangs from a tree. Black-eyed Susans massed at the "bottom" of the pocket almost obscure a narrow path leading to the President's House.

The Sue Schmidt Garden winds among the trees and grasses on one side of the Cherry Border. In the mottled shade, astilbes and Christmas ferns separate wide swaths of five different varieties of hostas. Spring brings a grand display of Yakusimanum rhododendrons, a very hardy, slow-growing variety named for the Japanese island where it originated. The aptly named cultivar 'Miss Maiden' blooms in a fresh and innocent apple-blossom white. In summer, a red-yellow-orange spectrum of daylilies flames the outer edge of this lovely garden.

Other special areas are the Harry Wood Garden, a quiet courtyard of rocks, shrubs, and ground covers; the James R. Frorer Holly Collection of over 200 varieties; the Dean Bond Rose Garden; and the Wister Garden.

The Wister Garden was created by the late Arboretum director in his backyard and an adjoining ravine. Many of the hybrid rhododendrons that form the background of the garden were developed at the Arboretum to extend the season of bloom. Along the upper level of the yard, a collection of 400 varieties of daffodils blooms from the beginning of April until early May. In early spring, Virginia bluebells and yellow wood poppies brighten the thinned woods of the ravine. Later, hostas, ferns, giant Jack-in-the-pulpits, hellebores, and the shiny black pea-sized fruits of jetbeads (*Rhodotypos scandens*) fill the landscape.

THE SCOTT ARBORETUM OF SWARTHMORE COLLEGE, Route 320, Swarthmore, PA 19081. (215) 328-8025.

OPEN
- Grounds, daily, dawn to dusk. No admission fee.
- Scott Offices, Monday to Friday, 8:30 A.M. to 4:30 P.M.

FACILITIES
Accessible to people with physical disabilities.

EVENTS
- Guided tours for groups with advance reservations. Admission fee.
- Courses, lectures, workshops on horticultural subjects; call Scott Offices for information, (215) 328-8025.

158

· Plant sale, September in odd-numbered years. The sale is held every other year because most of the hundreds of types of plants sold are propagated at the Arboretum and are not readily available at local nurseries.

DIRECTIONS
Lincoln Tunnel to New Jersey Turnpike south to Exit 6 to Pennsylvania Turnpike (Exit 6). Take Exit 24 and from the tollbooth go about 2 miles on I-76 to Route 320 south. Follow Route 320 about 14.5 miles to College Avenue. Turn right onto College Avenue. Scott Offices are 1 block ahead on the left.

SWISS PINES

MALVERN, PENNSYLVANIA

Swiss Pines is not Swiss at all, but a Japanese woodland garden. Gravel paths twist through a shady ravine, lush with plantings in cool, calming greens—the smoky bluish green of juniper and spruce; the inky green of yew. A Japanese threadleaf maple turns a diaphanous chartreuse in the sunlight. The surface of a pond is coated with velvety duckweed.

As in every Japanese garden, there are pools, watercourses, plantings, and rocks placed judiciously, each in balance and each symbolic. The garden is the world in microcosm; the paths, man's journey through life on an eternal quest for inner peace.

Revealed delights beckon. An arched bridge crosses to an island. There are a tea pavilion and a small Zen enclosure, its ground cover of white pebbles raked to perfection. Mossy stairs lead to a glass-enclosed miniature temple. But the entrance to these delights is barricaded with KEEP OUT signs. Ever-present arrows dictate where—and where not—to go.

Although the *raison d'être* of a Japanese garden is to induce a state of tranquillity, the barriers at Swiss Pines produce the opposite effect. A tantalizing invitation is offered, then withdrawn, inducing confusion, then annoyance. According to the garden's founder, Arnold Bartschi, the barriers became necessary to protect visitors from harming themselves and the garden, and to avoid possible legal suits.

Once you accept these Occidental barriers as a factor of the garden's transposition to contemporary western culture, you can contemplate some of the garden's exquisite details.

- At the entrance to the garden yellow bamboos, elegant and slender, flex ever so slightly in the breeze. High overhead the delicate slivers of leaves fracture the sunlight.
- The same leaf pattern is repeated in the ground cover of dwarf bamboo along many of the streams and ponds.
- The flow of water in a tiny brook is so regulated that the barest trickle of water just glazes the rocks and deepens the fringes of moss a deep sea green.
- A series of ponds are connected by an intricate network of water cascades and streamlets. Now you see it, now you don't. But the sound is always there—water purling, trickling, or surging until it comes to repose in a pool.
- White graveled cul-de-sacs overlook a teahouse, a pond, a glade, or a miniature valley. From the overlook the yews, hollies, and boxwoods look like green cylinders, hemispheres, giant ovals, serpentine mounds. A single Japanese maple shoots out a spray of ruby leaves over a sea of green.
- From a bamboo spout, drops of water spill into a basin. As one drop falls in, one drop spills out, an endless balance.

So on it goes. Typical of most Japanese gardens, the walk ends at a large pond that represents the sea, receiver of all waters and the end of the quest. A petite willow weeps on a petite peninsula. The backdrop to the pond is a very American open meadow starred with wildflowers on the other side of a fence. The contrast is a joyful celebration of two cultures side-by-side.

The garden's name—Swiss Pines—derives from its original owners, Arnold and Meta Bartschi, émigrés from Switzerland.

Mr. Bartschi made his fortune manufacturing children's shoes. The garden has long been his hobby, a distraction from business. How did he start? With a Japanese lantern, a bench, and a statue found under the 1800s farmhouse on his property. When he began, there were only open meadows, and four or five trees. He hired Katsuo Saito, premiere landscape architect from Japan, to design the garden. Saito came twice, each time for three weeks. Over the next 30 years the garden evolved. The 20 acres of Swiss Pines include the 9-acre Japanese woodland garden, 100 species of azaleas, a Bride's Walk (80 couples have been married at Swiss Pines), and a wildlife preserve, closed to the public.

SWISS PINES, The Arnold Bartschi Foundation, RD 1, Malvern, PA 19355. (215) 933-6916.

OPEN
March 15 through December 15, Monday through Friday, 10 A.M. to 4
P.M.; Saturday, 9 A.M. to 11 A.M. Closed holidays. No children under 12
permitted. No babies or toddlers, carried or in strollers. Shoes and
proper attire required. No admission fee.

FACILITIES
· Picnicking permitted in the parking lot.
· Garden not accessible to wheelchairs (gravel paths and steps).

DIRECTIONS
Lincoln Tunnel to New Jersey Turnpike south to Exit 6 to Pennsylvania
Turnpike. At Exit 24 (Valley Forge) take Route 23 north, going
through Port Kennedy. After Valley Forge the road becomes Nutt
Road. Take Nutt Road through Phoenixville. Beyond town at the
traffic light at the Fountain Inn, turn left onto Bridge Road, which
becomes Charlestown Road. Beyond the village of Charlestown about
½ mile on your right is the parking lot of Swiss Pines.

TEMPLE UNIVERSITY

The gardens of the horticulture department at Temple University are an educational doubleheader. There's a lot to look at and a lot to learn in the propagation greenhouses, identification gardens, a nursery, and the newest addition, an experimental wildflower meadow.

But best of all—a joy to see and the prime reason to visit Temple—is the newly renovated perennial garden, as English as Gertrude Jekyll. "Only we didn't plant goldenrod and corn in the same bed as she might have done," explains David Liscom, one of the two staff horticulturists (the other being Alice Bissell) who redeemed the garden.

Tattered and down on its luck after 50 years, the central garden mall had become an embarrassment. Despite severe budget limitations ($3,000), Liscom and Bissell undertook the renovation. They tore out ailing 25-year-old cherry trees and steam-cleaned the soil with a Rube Goldberg-like contraption Liscom rigged up. They swapped the use of a back hoe with the maintenance department for 400 begonia plants, begged trees from alumni now in the nursery business, and traded plants with Morris Arboretum.

After the steam-cleaning, the perennial beds were double dug to a depth of two feet, then made into raised beds.

In planning the perennial beds, one of the first things Liscom and Bissell did was to separate the two main functions of a teaching garden, display and identification. Aesthetically the two functions are incompatible when combined in one garden, since identification requires many one-of-a-kind species planted side by side.

Plant species were reduced from 100 to 65, and all one-of-a-kind plants eliminated. By massing fewer varieties according to color, form, or texture, Liscom and Bissell created an entirely different kind of garden.

The mall possessed some good, strong design elements—hemlock and arborvitae hedges that defined interior spaces and the edges of the garden, laid out in 1937 by two faculty members, husband and wife James and Louise Bush-Brown; and the stone garden house and fountain designed by Beatrix Jones Farrand at one end of the mall. Bissell and Liscom were stuck, however, with a massive, unshaded flagstone terrace that fronts a dormitory at the other end of the mall.

Within these parameters, the two began to plant their garden. Flowers are color coordinated by season, with only three major plant changes between April and September.

In spring, the primary colors dominate—hyacinths, daffodils, irises, pansies, and tulips. The tulip season is lengthened to eight weeks by replacing spent tulips with fresh bulbs kept dormant in a large storage refrigerator.

In summer, there are cool whites, pastel blues, and pinks of English daisies, blue salvia, snapdragons, begonias, and dusty miller. To add height, Liscom and Bissell planted summer-blooming delphinium, white "wedding" phlox, foxgloves, and pink hollyhocks that grow to 10 feet. For informality, the beds overrun with lupine, statice, baptisia (false indigo), ageratum, and alyssum.

In autumn, the garden blazes with pinks, purples, and golds. Tall

❧

PRECEDING PAGE: *One of the renovated beds of the perennial garden, looking toward the garden house designed by Beatrix Jones Farrand.*

pink asters replace the ragged pink hollyhocks. Asters range in color from smoke blue to royal purple. Gold, garnet, and rust mums are spiked with shasta daisies.

At the end of the perennial beds, the garden divides into two pocket gardens that are identical in size and shape. The similarity ends there. The two plots are a refreshing demonstration of how two very different gardens can be created by using different plant material.

One garden is planted with conifers in subdued shades of gray-green, dark green, and smoky blue. A champagne-colored threadleaf maple is set in a bed of purple ajuga. A dwarf Hinoki false cypress spreads its yellow-green fans against a gray stone wall. Wooden slab benches, weathered to silver gray, invite visitors to rest in this restrained, peaceful corner.

The other garden is planted with a confetti of flowers—zinnias, snapdragons, marigolds, and ruby red celosias. There is no seating. The garden is to be viewed in passing, like an Impressionist painting.

Other minigardens are divided by low cedar hedges and are differentiated by various geometric patterns of brick paving. These tiny plots—six in all—were planted by the winners of student design competitions sponsored by the horticulture department, a practice that the department plans to revive. The minigardens are fascinating studies in scale and proportion. In one plot tall, feathery fennel and dill stand, giraffelike, behind the low-growing sages, mints, and heathers in mottled shades of green. In another plot, a narrow frame of dwarf boxwood edges a solid square of saucy pink vincas, called 'Bright Eyes'.

A third plot is planted in pale green sage, purple-leaf basil, a mother-of-thyme which is dusty pink, and mauve garlic. Even a stump hosts mauve-colored fungus.

The formal garden of the central mall ends at a small forest, a belt 50 feet wide at most. A path winds through a wild tangle of ivy, ferns, and dogwoods growing under tulip trees. The woods serve as a buffer between the garden and a heavily traveled campus road, and as a backdrop for the Farrand-designed garden house and fountain.

The exit from the formal gardens is through an arch in a dense wall of Canadian hemlock. The arch makes a firm statement: you are leaving one environment, the formal gardens, for another—the working gardens.

The working gardens include the greenhouses and the identification beds of ornamental grasses, perennials, and annuals, with many varieties of each for comparison.

For example, one bed is planted with daylilies, natural miniatures alongside tetraploids. A tetraploid is a hybrid with a double set of chromosomes, which means more intense colors, more blooms. Left to their own devices, that is, sexually pollinated by bees, the offspring of the tetraploids will ultimately revert to the simple chromosomatic structure of one parent.

These beds are strictly business with anodized aluminum labels in BIG PRINT, so you do not have to stand on your head or lie down to read them.

The newest addition to Temple's horticultural complex is an experimental meadow planted with field flowers—"the hottest thing going these days," says Alice Bissell. "When the Minnesota Department of Transportation converted from grass to meadow, their maintenance costs—mostly for grass cutting—dropped from $68 million to $2 million a year."

In the Temple meadow, one part was disked (soil broken up by rotary disks), plowed, and then planted. A second part was disked, plowed, and treated with herbicide before planting. The third portion was sprayed in the spring of 1988 with a soap spray called Sharp Shooter, then disked and plowed. Results will determine future experimentation.

As the horticulture department expands from a two-year to a four-year program, the gardens will expand and change as well. Innovation is constant. "Besides, we have a long historical garden tradition here, with the Quakers and Pennsylvania Dutch," Alice Bissell concluded. "We have very sophisticated gardeners. They know and want quality. That keeps us hopping."

TEMPLE UNIVERSITY, Department of Horticulture, Ambler Campus, Butler Pike and Meetinghouse Road, Ambler, PA 19002. Greenhouse: (215) 283-1330.

OPEN
· Grounds, daily, 8 A.M. to dusk. No admission fee, but a parking permit is necessary, obtainable at the main administration building.
· Greenhouses, Monday through Friday, 8:30 A.M. to 4:30 P.M., except holidays.

FACILITIES
Not accessible to wheelchairs.

EVENTS
· Gardeners' Day, workshops, seminar, luncheon; last Saturday in May. Admission fee.

DIRECTIONS

Lincoln Tunnel to New Jersey Turnpike south to Exit 6 to Pennsylvania Turnpike, to Exit 26 (Ft. Washington Interchange). Go north on Route 309 about 3 miles, and exit left onto Susquehanna Road. At first traffic light, turn right onto Butler Pike, and go about ½ mile to Meetinghouse Road. Turn right onto Meetinghouse, and go ½ mile to campus entrance. Go first to the main administration building for parking permit.

WALLINGFORD
ROSE GARDENS

WALLINGFORD, PENNSYLVANIA

Among garden lovers there is a subspecies called rosarians, known to be impassioned, stubborn, and willful—people possessed. They have to be: they grow roses, America's national flower, a prima donna afflicted by every floral disease that comes by land, sea, and air. Devotion is a necessity.

To the Kassabs, Joseph and Betty, such devotion is a way of life. A note on their door greets visitors: "Don't be aggravated. We are probably in the garden." Probably? An understatement. In summer they live in their garden, which is the size of a tennis court, filled with roses.

No photograph will prepare you. Behind their big white-frame Victorian house, you enter the garden through a high, dense wall of Alberta spruce. Then the glory bursts upon you. Roses tumble down trellises 24 feet high in cascades of nacreous white, lemon, apricot, vermilion, garnet, fiery orange, champagne, and blush pink, 80 varieties of climbers, solid roses on three sides of the garden.

In the center, bed upon bed—seven rows in all—of hybrid teas blaze in sunset colors. Each is painstakingly disbudded so that only a few perfect, gargantuan roses grow on each stem.

To achieve this splendor, which runs from May through October, the Kassabs devote about three hours daily, dead-heading, weeding, watering. Midseason, Joe sprays every 7 to 10 days. Twice a year, he climbs a ladder to tie up the climbers with the precise knots of a surgeon, which he is.

Weeding is kept to a minimum by the pebbles that cover the beds. The Kassabs experimented with cocoa bean shells, which on a dewy morning made the garden smell like chocolate-covered roses. But the shells got washed away in a heavy rain. Now the Kassabs pack each bed to a depth of six inches with a layer of beige pebbles a half inch in diameter.

Joe embarked upon his lifelong passion for roses when he was six years old, earning 50¢ a day picking the petals of spent blossoms for a chemist who had planted roses in the early 1900s to test pesticides. Joe's family later purchased the house. Some of the original climbers are still there.

On their four acres, the Kassabs also grow specimen trees in an orchard that includes two katsuras that Admiral Dewey brought back from China in 1898, a dawn redwood, and a pair of "upright" English oaks, 25 years old and 40 feet tall, with only a 4-foot spread. The Kassabs specialize in hollies, doing a modest nursery business with them and with small Japanese maples.

The Kassabs rarely visit other gardens and never in summer. "I have to blindfold Joe to get him out of the driveway," says Betty. "Instead we show our garden. We work so hard at it. We want it to be seen."

And seen it is—by about 300 visitors each year.

WALLINGFORD ROSE GARDENS, Dr. Joseph and Betty Kassab, PO Box 52, Wallingford, PA 19086. (215) 566-2110.

OPEN
By appointment only. No admission fee.

FACILITIES
Limited accessibility for people with physical disabilities.

DIRECTIONS
Lincoln Tunnel to New Jersey Turnpike south to Exit 6 to Pennsylvania Turnpike, to Exit 24 (Valley Forge). Go south on Route 202 about 2½ miles to Route 252. Go south on Route 252 about 15 miles, passing through Newtown Square and Media. At the third traffic light beyond Media (Baltimore Pike is the first light), about 2 miles, turn left at Brookhaven Road. After approximately 150 feet, turn into first driveway on the right, through stone pillars with large lamps on top.

WEST LAUREL HILL
CEMETERY

BALA-CYNWYD, PENNSYLVANIA

Exuberant is not usually a word connected with graveyards, but that is the mood engendered by West Laurel Hill Cemetery, an expansive sweep of tomb, tree, and vista tucked in a bend of the Schuylkill River.

Laurel Hill is a garden of trees and monuments, larger-than-life marble statuary that glitters in the sun, and gargantuan trees. The trees were planted a century ago, one of every kind then known to withstand Philadelphia's winters, 150 species in all.

You will see trees in full regal glory as they are rarely seen. Each tree stands in splendid isolation, its texture and shape etched with a draftsman's precision against an open sweep of sky.

One magnolia (*Magnolia acuminata*) presides over the tomb of William Carpenter and his wife, Zipporah. What a memorial! This magnolia tree, also called cucumber tree for the shape of its fruit, stands 65 feet tall. Six leaves, some measuring two feet in length, are set in a starlike pattern on each stem. Green or gold according to season, the leaves clatter in a stiff breeze or waft gently like an elephant's ear, the patterns changing ceaselessly as breezes move across the foliage.

Wisps of Virginia creeper fall in single strands over a Gothic arch. Giant hydrangeas—mauve, of course, the preferred color of Victorians—"weep" over marble sarcophagi.

Alabaster angels, winged victories, obelisks—62 of them—are placed amid carefully arranged vistas. A weeping granite maid clings to an Adirondack rustic-style log cross. Ivy girdles marble urns.

The Biddles are buried here, as is Harry Wright, the father of baseball. His statue is mounted on a granite base embellished with two crossed bats and a ball. Sarah Hale, author of "Mary Had a Little Lamb," has her poem enscribed on her tombstone.

Laurel Hill originally was "a gentleman's country estate" four miles upriver from Philadelphia. In 1835 it was purchased for a cemetery site by influential citizens for two purposes. Its rural location would remove the danger of disease spreading from bodies buried hastily in shallow graves in a densely populated area. And it would provide the bereaved with uplifting scenic views from which to contemplate the sublimity of God and nature. Laurel Hill was not only to be a final resting place, but a place of joyous communion, the living with the dead.

So here for more than a century the Main Line has buried its first families—in mausoleums lined up like sugar cubes, each with a different architectural facade. There are Moorish, Gothic, and Greek temple "fronts." One family crypt is a miniature Parthenon, another a Theban pyramid. One four-spired confection looks startlingly like Queen Victoria's memorial to Prince Albert in London. Heavy metal doors are in Gaudian, Byzantine, and art nouveau styles.

The funerary sculpture, most of it marble, takes on a life of its own, becoming nacreous lemon-tinted at dawn, flat white in the noonday sun, roseate gold at sunset, and sullen gray under a cloudy sky.

Because it is beautiful, and because rural cemeteries were the landscape models for the great public parks that followed in the nineteenth century—these are the reasons to visit Laurel Hill.

Listed in the National Register of Historic Places, Laurel Hill is the second oldest rural cemetery in America. (Mt. Auburn in Boston

❧

PRECEDING PAGE: *West Laurel Hill, America's second oldest rural cemetery, in a 1913 photograph.*

opened in 1831.) Its carriage roads loop 100 acres of hill and ravine. By a 1987 count, there have been 70,000 interments, with enough places left to last another 90 years. Plots in this garden of earthly triumph range from $655 (for 2) to $60,000 (for 20) in a "feature" lot, which means a lot with a view or special plantings or in a rockery. If you plan to plant your own tree, a small extra endowment is required.

WEST LAUREL HILL CEMETERY COMPANY, 215 Belmont Avenue, Bala-Cynwyd, PA 19004. (215) 664-1591.

OPEN
· Monday through Saturday, 8 A.M. to 4 P.M.; Sunday and holidays, 9 A.M. to 4 P.M.
· Tours, limited to 25, arranged in advance; no admission fee.

FACILITIES
Accessible to people with physical disabilities; paved roads on much of the grounds, with heavy automobile traffic at times.

DIRECTIONS
Lincoln Tunnel to New Jersey Turnpike south to Exit 3 (Runnemede). From exit ramp take Route 168 north (Black Horse Pike). Proceed north about 3½ miles. Follow sign in right lane to South Philadelphia/ Walt Whitman Bridge. Exit from bridge onto Route 76 west; go about 7 miles to Exit 31 (City Avenue) (exit is from left lane). Travel on City Avenue for about 5 traffic lights to Belmont Avenue (there is a shopping center at the intersection). Turn right onto Belmont; after second intersection, look for large entrance gate on right.

WINTERTHUR

WINTERTHUR, DELAWARE

Winterthur is most famous for its collection of American decorative arts, one of the most prestigious in the world, assembled by Henry Francis du Pont over half a century.

Lesser known is Henry du Pont's second passion, his gardens, almost 1,000 acres of meadow, forest, and specialty planting areas.

From the visitors' center in the middle of a shallow valley, a 360-degree pastoral panorama unfolds, frame by frame. You see gentle hills, and ponds afloat with ducks and geese. Daffodils sweep across a meadow above Clenny Run as it meanders its way to the Brandywine River, 1½ miles distant. A huge ruffle of pink, salmon, and orchid azaleas decorates a draw between two hills. In the distance, slate barn roofs glitter in the sun. A forest of century-old trees frames ice white rhododendrons.

Du Pont loved greens and pastels, so that is the prevailing palette of Winterthur. His sense of color was delicate and sure. Ribbons of color—pale pinks, peach, mauve, lavender, blue—stream across a meadow or down a ravine. Ivory blends into blush pink, then into orchid, which melds into deep lilac. Colors gather intensity as they move down a hill. Occasional bright slashes of color are artfully deployed as accents, to define the entrance to a garden area or frame a vista. A burgundy cutleaf maple, planted next to an apricot-colored azalea marks a turn in the path. A fringe of dogwood threads its way under a row of dark green conifers.

Of Winterthur's 963 acres, 60 are planted intensively as specialty gardens, each defined by its name: Peony Garden, Azalea Walk, Magnolia Bend, Winter-Hazel Area, Pinetum, Sycamore Area, Oak Hill, and March Bank. They weave easily among one another, connected by a macadam road. Side tributaries—footpaths of tanbark and gravel—lace through woodland glades.

Winterthur for all its vast magnitude is a simple, naturalistic garden, its simplicity carefully nurtured by its creator, Henry du Pont. No trees at Winterthur are trimmed into topiary shapes. There are no formal allées and few man-made architectural features. Du Pont tampered little with the natural contours of the land, but he did dam Clenny's Run to make four ponds. After his death, an abandoned quarry, wet with seeping springs, was converted into a rock garden. Rock slabs were brought from other parts of the estate to "refurbish" this rocky cul-de-sac. But that is the extent of the land alteration. What a contrast to the lavish gardens built by his cousins, Pierre at Longwood, Alfred at Nemours, and, to a lesser extent, by his sister at Louise's Folly at Eleutherian Mills!

Simple as this naturalistic landscape appears, it—and the house—required the work of 250 employees and the complex planning and constant vigilance of du Pont. But then he was a perfectionist.

In spring, when houseguests were in residence, du Pont kept 20 gardeners on call to move full-blooming azalea bushes to fill out ragged or empty spots.

In the natural forest, trees were—and still are—coddled with lightning rods, surgery, and trussed as needed. To stabilize one grand old sycamore, 17 tons of concrete were poured down its central rotting core. Such a practice is now outmoded, but the sycamore stands alive, a lone giant in a meadow named after it.

To soften the edges of a 10-hole golf course, du Pont planted large circles and arcs of daffodils, always planting just one species or a single color in one place for uniform impact. When the daffodils were in bloom, golfers were forbidden to whack their ball out of the daffodil rough. The daffodil patches were considered worse than sand traps.

For 65 years, du Pont supervised plantings set out according to a very exacting plan. He limited plant materials, preferring flowering shrubs, mostly rhododendrons, azaleas, dogwoods, and quince. After ferreting out a unique species, he would test it for three years for color, hardiness, and the length of its blooming period, then propagate the most spectacular performers. Only then would a shrub take its honored place on a hillside.

Although as many as 25,000 daffodil bulbs might be planted in one season, du Pont recorded their placement. This was no small task, considering that bulbs were set among gnarled tree roots according to a seemingly random pattern, but achieved by placing a large tree branch on the ground and planting bulbs along the line of the limbs.

In September of 1911, he gave to his cousin Anna Robinson full directions for the fall planting:

> I should be very grateful if you would undertake to superintend the planting of these bulbs. . . . All you need to do is walk over the sloping bank looking for wooden labels with names corresponding to those on the list. . . . If by some mistake there should not be enough bulbs to fill the required spaces, simply omit planting one of them, but kindly mention the fact on a little label. The bank, of course, in addition to the spaces marked, is full of labels of bulbs already planted there and, naturally, these must not be disturbed.

At the end of her task, Anna reported, "The relief is intense. . . ."

Du Pont plotted the blooming sequence of his flowers with equal precision, seeking species that would extend the season, such as early and late lilacs, or one of Winterthur's earliest blooming azaleas, a purple-speckled émigré from high mountain slopes in China. Under giant tulip trees, beeches, and oaks, swaths of Virginia bluebells flow like rivers in early spring. As their blossoms wane, the later-flowering Spanish bluebells take their place.

Such intensive orchestration exacts a price. A kind of mechanistic perfection lays its hand upon Winterthur. Nothing has been left to chance. No spontaneity, no brilliant accidents mar this even-keeled garden, as emotionally cool as its colors.

Du Pont's professional preferences were clearly apparent. He chose to study horticulture, not landscape architecture. Above all, he was a plantsman. Some of his most treasured hours at Winterthur were spent filling notebook after notebook with his observations about plant life, not sketches of garden designs.

Born at Winterthur in 1880, he grew up under the stern direction of a military father, Henry Algernon du Pont, a graduate of West Point. Called the Colonel, he admonished his son always to bring honor to the family name. Together father and son tramped the woods and planted the fine specimen trees in the Pinetum. On strolls with his children, the

Colonel would drill them on the Latin names of plants. If they failed to answer correctly, they were sent to bed without dinner.

A shy, lonely boy, Henry was sent off to Groton at the age of 13. After graduating from Harvard's horticultural school, the now defunct Bussey Institution, he came home to manage the family farm and prize herd of Holstein-Friesian cows.

When the Colonel died in 1926, Henry was 46 years old, free at last to indulge his two passions, his gardens and collecting American decorative arts. Both his time and his funds were virtually unlimited.

Up every morning at six o'clock, du Pont breakfasted on hot water and lemon juice. Not until lunchtime at one o'clock did he cease his round of activities—inspecting the gardens, conferring with gardeners in the production greenhouses, corresponding with horticulturists. Year by year, plant by plant, the gardens expanded to 11 major areas.

Of these areas, only two are formal gardens—the Sundial Garden, built on the site of a tennis court, and the Reflecting Pool Garden, incorporating the former family swimming pool. Both were designed by Marian Coffin, a longtime family friend who had studied landscape architecture at MIT when du Pont was at Harvard.

Below the house, now a museum, the Reflecting Pool Garden is a garden-in-a-glade, a small, delicate, reclusive haven done in the style of a walled Italian Renaissance garden.

Halfway down a long flight of stone stairs, an iron arch, festooned with ivy, frames the reflecting pool. It is flanked by two stone garden houses with steep red-tiled roofs. Water jets on either side of a bronze horse spout small streams into the pool. The sound of water fracturing the glassy black surface dominates this verdant, peaceful garden. Terra-cotta jardinieres planted with pink hydrangeas and asparagus vines are set along a low stone wall. Iron gates open to woods carpeted with tiny blue glory-of-the-snows (*Chionodoxa*). Frogs duck under duckweed, and golden carp move lazily through two small ponds.

The other formal garden, very different in mood, is located on a sun-drenched hillside, with plantings faithful to du Pont's color pallette. The Sundial Garden is cradled in a large grassy saucer with a wall of dark green behind it—extraordinarily tall firs, pines, and cedars, many planted by the Colonel over a century ago. The wiry needled branches of two blue Atlas spruce dominate the wall of green.

A bronze sundial sits in the middle, oxidized to the same bluish green as the spruce. Around the sundial, a low, matted bed of honeysuckle privet flops its shaggy dark green against the fine-textured lawn. From the saucer, pastels ranging from orchid to chartreuse layer up the gentle hillside, beginning with lilac bushes, then salmon-flowering quinces, and snowy almonds. In the last show of spring color, snowball viburnums and white crab apple blossoms bloom overhead. A few weeks later, the blossoms of the empress trees will replace the lavender of the lilacs.

A prudent man, Henry du Pont perceived early that suburban Wilmington could sprawl its way to Winterthur. In 1969 he granted long-term leases on 2,400 acres to a Methodist retirement home, the Wilmington Country Club, and Brandywine State Park. As a result of these additional adjacent buffers, Winterthur is one of the few public gardens where quiet prevails, broken only by the occasional loudspeaker of the garden tram. It is an equitable trade-off. The tram carries 8,000 people a year who could not otherwise hike the hillsides and ravines.

Henry du Pont has been dead two decades. In a book about Winterthur in 1985, his two daughters wrote touchingly of their memories.

> What do we, the children of Henry Francis du Pont, remember about Winterthur? First is the outdoors, the swaying watercress in Clenny Run Creek, mint and forget-me-nots, bunches of which we picked for our mother's birthday every year. On the hills and meadows were dandelions, Queen Anne's lace, clover, and daisies that we often plucked and then left behind under our swings when the morning was over. . . . The presiding genius of our surroundings was our father . . . Henry Francis du Pont loved Winterthur. It was his achievement, his birthplace, his home, and the place where he died. His enthusiasm for the house, the museum, and the land speaks to us still.
>
> RUTH ELLEN DU PONT LORD
> PAULINE LOUISE DU PONT HARRISON

WINTERTHUR MUSEUM AND GARDENS, Winterthur, DE 19735. (302) 888-4600.

OPEN
- Museum and gardens, daily, Tuesday through Saturday, 9 A.M. to 5 P.M.; Sunday, noon to 5 P.M.; closed Mondays, New Year's Day, Easter, Thanksgiving, December 24, and Christmas. Admission fee.
- Visitors' Pavilion, Tuesday through Saturday, 8:30 A.M. to 5 P.M.; Sunday, 11 A.M. to 5 P.M.

FACILITIES
- Garden Cafeteria; Restaurant at Winterthur.
- Gallery Café (open seasonally for outdoor dining).
- Garden Shop.
- Gallery Shops—reproduction furniture, fabrics, decorative accessories.
- Winterthur Bookstore and Sugarplum Shop.
- Picnic House.
- House and gardens fully accessible to wheelchairs, available without additional charge.

EVENTS
- Garden tram tour (weather permitting), mid-April through mid-November on all days the museum and gardens are open. No admission fee between June 2 and November 15.
- Garden Walks, guided tours for groups of 10, March through mid-November, twice daily; reservations suggested. Admission fee.
- Point-to-Point Race: horse racing, pony racing, parade of antique carriages, first Sunday in May.
- Yuletide at Winterthur, rooms decorated for historical holiday entertaining, mid-November to end of December.
- Music at Winterthur, Delaware Symphony Orchestra and preconcert dinners, three Friday evenings, one in November, one in January, and one in March. Admission fee.

DIRECTIONS
Lincoln Tunnel to New Jersey Turnpike south to Delaware Memorial Bridge. Take I-295 north, through Wilmington, to Route 52. Take Route 52 north 6 miles. Gate is on right.

CONNECTICUT

THE BARTLETT
ARBORETUM

STAMFORD, CONNECTICUT

The Bartlett Arboretum is down a narrow wooded road in the middle of a moneyed Connecticut suburb. There are no guards, no closed gates, no attendants, not even many people—just 63 acres of pleasure, including woodland trails, specimen trees, rhododendrons, azaleas, perennials, wildflowers, flowering trees, and dwarf conifers.

If you haven't been exposed to dwarf conifers before, Bartlett's collection could be the first to spark a grand passion. (The word *dwarf* means a slow-growing cultivar of a species, not something that will necessarily stay small forever.) The colors—golden green, gray-blue, and malachite—are sensual; so are the shapes and textures. The conifers sprawl, mound, or stand erect. Their needles range from long and languid to short and stubby.

Some dwarf conifers are common, some rare, but all are pieces of sculpture. Some look like stacks of ruffled green petticoats. From a distance, an Alberta spruce appears solid; up close, the fine needles form a delicate, compact pattern like frost on a winter's window.

About 150 dwarf conifer cultivars are set in irregularly shaped beds. Paths wander over hillocks and climb above a stone retaining wall. Because of these hilly contours, the garden appears much larger than one acre. From one side, with an aged crab apple in the center, two pines frame a view across the garden to the woods on the opposite side.

Planted near the entrance to the Arboretum is a cluster of dwarf evergreens produced from the seeds of witches'-brooms. Some of these striking, shrublike "mounds" are waist-high, so dense that no light can be seen through them. One flops barely eight inches off the ground. Witches'-brooms are mutations, thick abnormal growths that sometimes develop on conifers and that are genetically different from the parent. Botanists don't know why. The intriguing feature is that witches'-brooms can be propagated as new evergreen varieties.

In the Plant Science Department of the University of Connecticut, Dr. Sidney Waxman has been growing witches'-broom seedlings to produce new dwarf varieties since 1963. A population grown from witches'-broom seeds will be half-dwarf, half-normal (like the host tree). From the dwarf half, Dr. Waxman grows about 20,000 seedlings at a time, observing them for 7 to 10 years in all seasons, constantly eliminating until only the best are left.

The best means good color—green, blue, or golden yellow; dense branching; short needles; good form; different, less symmetric shapes; and easy to propagate. "I'm very picky about choosing one to propagate," Dr. Waxman says. "So far I've only found about 15 witches'-brooms good enough to name, like 'Green Shadow' and 'Blue Shag'." The named varieties are given, free, to commercial propagators.

Witches'-brooms derive their name from old wives' tales. According to one story, when a spirit leaves the body of an evil person at the cemetery, it is prevented from reaching heaven by getting stuck in the branches of a tree. The entrapped spirit becomes a witches'-broom. Or, in the more obvious tale, the growths are brooms for witches to fly on.

Fact or fable, a high percentage of witches'-brooms *is* found in cemeteries. That's where Dr. Waxman found 12 of his first 30 specimens. Once, along the Rhode Island shore, he spotted a broom

❧

PRECEDING PAGE: *The dwarf conifer garden.*

high in a distant tree. He tracked it down and found a concrete marker at the base of the tree, inscribed BUSTER, OUR DOG. (If you see a witches'-broom growing in a tree, let Dr. Waxman know, and he will send you an "official" witches'-broom-spotter certificate.)

Other cultivated areas in the Arboretum include an allée of Eastern red cedars underplanted with hostas; a rectangle of pollarded trees (cut back to the trunk so the foliage grows in a dense head); and a secluded garden of blue and white flowers—prairie gentians (*Eustoma grandiflorum*, usually labeled *Lisianthus*), nicotiana, delphiniums, and salvias—ringed by azaleas and rhododendrons. A large perennial border is spiced by a long-blooming range of cultivars that goes well beyond those usually seen in public gardens.

Almost every single growing thing at the Bartlett Arboretum is labeled, even the many daylily varieties in the perennial border. This is a precious boon to plant lovers and too rare in even the best public gardens.

In the woodlands, well-marked trails traverse a natural forest of oak, maple, and hickory, and a swamp habitat of black gum, cardinal flowers, and skunk cabbage.

Some of the older trees in the Arboretum were planted by Dr. Francis A. Bartlett, founder of the Bartlett Tree Expert Company, which still has headquarters in Stamford. The Bartletts lived here in the 1920s and 1930s, while the company used the woodlands for experimental and research work. Bartlett experimented with grafting—he made a branch grow upside down and grew pears on a mountain ash.

In 1965 the company's tree laboratory moved to North Carolina to escape Connecticut taxes. After a citizens' campaign raised the necessary funds, the state took over the property, now under the administration of the University of Connecticut.

THE BARTLETT ARBORETUM, 151 Brookdale Road, Stamford, CT 06903-4199. (203) 322-6971.

OPEN
- Grounds, daily, 8:30 A.M. to sunset. No admission fee.
- Greenhouse, "most days," 9:30 A.M. to 11:30 A.M.
- Administration building, Monday to Friday, 8:30 A.M. to 4 P.M., and some weekends for special events.

FACILITIES
Limited accessibility for people with physical disabilities; dirt paths.

183

EVENTS
· Winter Bloom Day, a Sunday in February, bulbs and different flowers forced each year in the greenhouse, display and sale. No admission fee.
· Annual plant sale, first Saturday in May.

DIRECTIONS
Triborough Bridge to Bruckner Expressway (I-278) to Hutchinson River Parkway north to Merritt Parkway to Exit 35. Go north on High Ridge Road (Route 137) 1.6 miles to Brookdale Road. Turn left onto Brookdale, and Bartlett is about ½ mile ahead on the right.

CAPRILANDS HERB FARM

The gardens at Caprilands are as American as a crazy quilt and as down-home as their ebullient, colorful owner, Adelma Simmons.

There are 30 gardens in all, small plots that run in zigzag shapes. Flowers overrun weathered wood or brick borders. In the rose garden, poison ivy girdles an ancient apple tree.

Adelma has given the garden plots snappy names like Garden of the Stars, Pipers Garden, and Thyme Terrace. Then there are the color gardens—gold, silver, and blue.

In the Bride's Garden, forget-me-nots, heart-shaped ivy, and lemon verbena (also called bride's sachet), fill two heart-shaped plots edged in brick. Orange trees, whose blossoms symbolize virginity and fertility, are set out in terra-cotta tubs, and there is myrtle, which is traditionally woven into bridal crowns. But brides beware. Adelma's garden book relates that myrtle will wither on any but a virginal brow.

Garden Tinctoria contains such dye plants as smoke tree, weld, poke, and woad, a major source of indigo before Germany discovered its synthetic counterpart in the late 1890s.

The Saints Garden is bisected by cross-shaped beds of thyme, edged with white stones. Madonna lilies grow at the foot of a small statue of the Virgin Mary. Angelica, crown-of-thorns, monkshood, and

Jacob's-ladder are all there, as is Mary's gold, a wild calendula of Sicily reputed to bloom on all of Mary's holy days.

Labels are pure homespun Adelma. In the Saints Garden they are written on black slate slabs. One reads: A FIG TREE—MAN'S FIRST CLOTHING. In the Identification Garden labels for herbs and vegetables are written on wooden kitchen spoons and stuck in the soil. So are the labels for gallon jugs of vinegar—basil, dill, tarragon—that lie on the ground seasoning in the sun. The vinegars will be bottled and sold in the Caprilands gift shop.

A meticulous gardener Adelma is not; a raconteur she is. Standing still as a bee skep (a dome-shaped hive) in her garden, she shakes her red corkscrew curls and philosophizes about plants, people, and life. "You keep changing things, that's what you do," she advises. "A little here, a little there. I am in the garden every morning by 7:30. I look a calendula in the face. How can you be unhappy when you look a calendula in the face? Then I stroll. What flower beds to rip out? What to put in the window boxes this week? No garden looks the same two days in a row. Change keeps you young. When you fear change, you fear life."

Adelma has been about this garden business—and business is what Caprilands is all about—for 60 years. She and her parents bought the stony, arid 100 acres in 1929. Automobiles rusted in the meadow, and chickens roosted in the farmhouse. The family raised dairy cows (unsuccessfully); then goats (somewhat successfully). When Adelma started to grow herbs, only onions and garlic were regularly stocked in larders for seasoning. Today her best-seller, *Herb Gardening in Five Seasons*, is in its eighteenth printing.

Each midday at Caprilands 75 guests are served luncheon in the eighteenth-century farmhouse, overflowing with antiques and flowers. They dine on nasturtium blossom salad and parsley-onion squares washed down with May wine spiked with sweet woodruff—the ingredients all grown in Caprilands' gardens.

Home gardeners and cooks will find much value in Adelma's barn lectures and books. Businessmen will learn a thing or two about showmanship from the flower and gift shops. Everyone will have his spirits lifted, for above all, Caprilands is fun.

CAPRILANDS HERB FARM, 534 Silver Street, Coventry, CT 06238. (203) 742-7244.

OPEN
Garden and shops, daily, 9 A.M. to 5 P.M., except New Year's Day, Easter, Thanksgiving, and Christmas. No admission fee.

FACILITIES
- Restaurant, in an eighteenth-century farmhouse, open for lunch only (reservations necessary) and for special teas.
- Picnicking permitted in limited places upon request.
- Gift, book, and plant shops.
- Greenhouse gallery.
- Limited accessibility to wheelchairs; paths are paved, grass, and gravel; a few front steps to house.

EVENTS
- Daily luncheon programs include a garden tour and barn lecture at noon on all aspects of gardening, its history, cooking and decorating with herbs and flowers. Many special holiday and festival programs with music: Midsummer Festival, last week in June; Lammas Harvest Festival, late July and early August; St. Fiacres Day, August 30; Michelmas Days in mid-September. Phone reservations necessary for lunch, which includes programs. Admission fee.
- Sunday teas, April through mid- to late December. Admission fee.

DIRECTIONS
Henry Hudson Parkway north to Saw Mill River Parkway to I-84 east past Hartford to Exit 59. Turn onto Route 384 and go about 7 miles to the end. Turn east onto Route 44. Go about 3¼ miles, and turn right onto Silver Street. Entrance is on right, about 1 mile.

HARKNESS MEMORIAL STATE PARK

WATERFORD, CONNECTICUT

On a breezy promontory overlooking Long Island Sound, where the Pequot Indians once held summer encampments, philanthropist Edward S. Harkness developed the family's 234-acre summer estate. He named it Eolia for the mythical god of the winds. Great sweeps of open lawn roll down to the water. Nothing mars the views of the sea from the massive 42-room limestone mansion.

The entire park and the three gardens around the mansion—the Italian west garden, the Oriental east garden, and the rock garden—are being restored as they were when the Harknesses lived at Eolia.

In 1919 Harkness hired the noted landscape designer Beatrix Jones Farrand to revamp the planting of the Italian west garden. Working with the existing garden (the limestone pergola and the shape of the beds had been set in place 13 years before), Farrand planted a subdued palette of blues, soft oranges, yellows, and touches of mauve and—very sparingly—white. In the current restoration, her plantings will be recreated with perennials grouped by color, one species to a four-foot area.

For 16 years, Farrand was a familiar figure at Eolia, keeping an eye on the gardens. She designed the rock garden and the stone path that ran like an ancient streambed between spreads of golden lady's-slippers and other wildflowers. Through the years subsequent gardeners added a crosshatch of paths, which now will be eliminated. Other infidelities, like Mary Harkness's monogram in privet, will be removed and replaced with plants that can be seen in family photographs from the 1930s.

Farrand also designed the Oriental east garden. Her original structures—the surrounding stone walls, the Chinese and Korean statues, the sunken middle section of the garden, and the pool—still remain.

But the restored plantings will be those of Marian Coffin, another landscape architect hired by Harkness in 1949 to refurbish the east garden. At that time Coffin, who had worked on Henry du Pont's Winterthur and many Long Island estates, chose a planting scheme in a soothing Gertrude Jekyll-like watercolor of lavenders, pinks, and whites.

Thus the restoration of the gardens will show the work of both women. By 1990 the perennials will be blooming in their proper places.

Harkness could well afford this mile of fine-sand beachfront—his father had loaned John D. Rockefeller $60,000 to help start Standard Oil and was his silent partner over the years. Harkness and his wife, Mary, were generous, giving $200 million to philanthropies ranging from buildings at Yale University to providing radios for lightship crews and tenders. Mrs. Harkness bequeathed Eolia to the state of Connecticut.

The restored mansion is scheduled to reopen in 1990, furnished with English, American, and Chinese furniture similar to that owned by the Harknesses.

HARKNESS MEMORIAL STATE PARK, Great Neck Road, Waterford, CT 06385. (203) 443-5725.

OPEN
- Park, every day, 8 A.M. to sunset. Parking fee.
- Greenhouse, daily, Memorial Day through Labor Day, 10 A.M. to 5 P.M.

FACILITIES
- Picnicking and fishing permitted.
- Limited accessibility to people with physical disabilities; some steps.

EVENTS
- Classical concerts, under a tent on the lawn, 6 Saturdays in July and August. Admission fee.
- Midweek jazz concerts, July and August. Admission fee.
- Children's concerts, 2 summer Saturdays. No admission fee.

DIRECTIONS

Triborough Bridge to Bruckner Expressway (I-278) to New England Thruway (I-95) north to Exit 74. Go south on Route 161 about 3 miles to the end. Turn left onto Route 156, and go about 2½ miles to Route 213 (Great Neck Road). Turn right onto Route 213, and go about 3 miles to Harkness on the right.

HILLSIDE GARDENS

NORFOLK, CONNECTICUT

Hillside Gardens is the backyard garden and commercial nursery of uncommon perennials owned by Fred and Mary Ann McGourty. The four acres of gardens are dazzling, with long beds and borders of perennials, some cut into the lawn, others planted along stone walls.

Ferns and other shade-loving perennials grow along a path leading into the woods. Ornamental vegetables in a curved bed look good enough to eat. Flowers are tucked into the crevices of stone steps and in wooden tubs around the house. Hillside looks like what it is: a garden of passionate and sophisticated plantspeople.

"Our location is so remote [northeastern Connecticut]," says Fred McGourty, "that we need to stress the uncommon to get people here." To find the uncommon, the McGourtys search the seed lists of the American Rock Garden Society, the Royal Horticultural Society, the Hardy Plant Society. They travel to Europe to find new plants. When the plants do well in their own backyard, they propagate and sell them. In a sense, Hillside is a trial garden to see what works.

Here is a sampling of the uncommon perennials grown at Hillside: *Knautia macedonica,* a dark crimson pincushion of a flower that blooms all summer in a sheltered alcove of the McGourtys' 200-year-old farmhouse; *Veronicastrum virginicum* 'Alba-roseum', whose pinkish

191

white racemes waft four feet high over dark green foliage; and *Strobilanthes atropurpureus*, big and bushy and covered with small deep purple-blue flowers.

Hillside is a garden of ideas, a place to see how plants work together, how a perennial in a six-inch pot will look as a mature plant. For example, helenium 'Copper Spray' grows into a five-foot fireball of copper-colored flowers that blooms into October.

The airy white candelabrumlike flowers of black cohosh (*Cimicifuga racemosa*) reach seven feet, blooming from early July to early August. After the flowers have gone to seed, the green stems still lend height and pattern to the border, fulfilling one McGourty criterion of a "good" perennial—summerlong performance of either flower or foliage.

Another criterion is the ability of a plant to extend the season beyond summer, into late fall—or longer, like sedum 'Autumn Joy' with rust-colored dead flower heads that look good all winter. Or the 30 kinds of grasses at Hillside, which turn from tawny to parchment color, carry well into March, and after being cut down, provide new growth in summer.

The curved flower bed behind the house is Hillside's showcase. A low stone wall divides the bed into shady and sunny areas. On the sunny side are the blues of veronica, monkshood, and globe thistle; the pinks and scarlet of bee balm, astilbe, and phlox; the yellows of potentilla, meadow rue (*Thalictrum speciosissimum*), and heliopsis; the white of feverfew. On the shady side, hostas, daylilies, ferns, and lungwort grow under three blue spruces and a dwarf Alberta spruce.

Throughout Hillside, plantings soften the strong lines of stone walls that bound and cross the property, relics of a turn-of-the-century dairy farm.

Fred McGourty was editor of the Brooklyn Botanic Garden pioneer handbook series when he began gardening seriously on weekends at Hillside in the 1960s. He and Mary Ann started a weekend nursery in 1979 for added income, and in four years, the nursery became a full-time venture. They now grow 80 percent of the plants they sell, particularly the unusual varieties.

The McGourtys also design and install gardens from southern Vermont to the outskirts of New York City. Landscaping is now half of their business. And they write. Two of their current titles are *Perennials—How to Select, Grow & Enjoy*, by Fred McGourty and Pamela Harper, and *Ground Covers, Vines and Ornamental Grasses*, edited by Mary Ann McGourty.

"Mary Ann and I have an arrangement," Fred explains. "One

winter she cooks and I write, and the next winter we reverse it. The cooking is easy."

HILLSIDE GARDENS, PO Box 614, 515 Litchfield Road, Norfolk, CT 06058. (203) 542-5345.

OPEN
Nursery and gardens, daily, except holidays, May through September, 9 A.M. to 5 P.M. No admission fee.

FACILITIES
· Perennials and McGourty books are for sale.
· Limited accessibility for people with physical disabilities; grass paths, one or two steps.

DIRECTIONS
Triborough Bridge to Bruckner Expressway (I-278) to Hutchinson River Parkway north to I-684 to the end. Take Route 84 east to Waterbury, then Route 8 north to Torrington. From Torrington, go west on Route 4 for about 2 miles to Route 272 (there is a gas station on the right). Turn right (north) on Route 272, and go about 10 miles. Just past Dennis Hill State Park, Hillside is on the right.

WESTERN
MASSACHUSETTS

BERKSHIRE GARDEN CENTER

STOCKBRIDGE, MASSACHUSETTS

Since 1934, the not-for-profit Berkshire Garden Center has been a splendid horticultural resource with 15 acres of landscaped gardens, a pond, an orchard, a wildflower meadow, greenhouses, horticultural exhibitions, a library and bookshop, and enthusiastic volunteers ready to dispense advice and encouragement.

By the mid-1980s, the center was in a serious slump. Grounds were ragged. Plants begged for maintenance.

After looking at slides of their garden of yesteryear, the Board of Directors was shocked at the deterioration. In 1988 they devised a five-year plan of revitalization. Since the owners of vacation homes are now a major economic force in the Berkshires, the plan emphasizes, among other things, low-maintenance plantings for absentee gardeners.

The Center is worth a visit, in part because the basic plantings and terrain are interesting—rocky outcroppings, a meadow of primroses, pear trees bedded in forget-me-nots—and in part because under its five-year plan the garden is beginning to flourish again.

BERKSHIRE GARDEN CENTER, Stockbridge, MA 01262. (413) 298-3926.

OPEN

Garden, shops, greenhouse, daily, 10 A.M. to 5 P.M., May 1 to mid-October. Office, 10 A.M. to 5 P.M., daily except all legal holidays.

FACILITIES

· Reference library.
· Picnicking permitted.
· Garden, gift, and herb shops.
· Accessible to wheelchairs. Paths are mostly grass and gravel with steps or slopes between grade levels. Golf cart available upon request.

EVENTS

· Daffodil Show, weekend in late April.
· Mai-Bowle Open House, Sunday in early May.
· Potting Day, weekend in early May.
· Plant Fair, weekend in mid-May.
· Herb Fair, Saturday in mid-June.
· Antique Show, weekend in early July.
· Flower Show, weekend in mid-August.
· Annual Harvest Festival, late September.
· Christmas workshops, early December.

DIRECTIONS

Henry Hudson Parkway north to Saw Mill River Parkway to Taconic State Parkway. Go to the end, and pick up Massachusetts Turnpike east to Lee/Stockbridge exit. Take Route 102 south out of Stockbridge. Go 3 miles. The center is at the junction of routes 102 and 183.

CHESTERWOOD

The garden at Chesterwood is simplicity itself, a restful green space enclosed on three sides by hemlocks and ancient lilacs. This grassy rectangle is intersected by two gravel paths that cross at a circular fountain.

The simplicity of the garden and its importance in the life of Daniel Chester French are the reasons to visit Chesterwood. French, one of America's most beloved sculptors, planned his garden as an extension of his studio. Here, for 35 summers—from 1896 until his death in 1931—French translated the patriotic sentiments of Victorian America into national monuments. His most famous are the Minute Man at Concord, Massachusetts, the statue of Lincoln in the Lincoln Memorial, and Columbia University's seated female, Alma Mater.

French believed that gardens were like sculpture, that their success depended on their foundation. "If skeleton and bones are in the right places," he once wrote, "then chances are you'd have a statue or a garden that would stand up and look well through the years."

The skeleton of French's garden was in the right place, and it endures as the cheery, inviting, livable space French intended.

The skeleton is the central courtyard, which his daughter once described as "a room of living green with seats in the shade in the right places"; the woods that define the garden perimeter; the paths that anchor the studio to the garden; and the architectural features that define major intersections—fluted columns and an iron archway that flank the paths where they enter the woods; and the circular fountain and marble bench in front of the studio.

The view of the garden from the studio was one of French's favorites and one he sketched many times. The plantings are historically correct, much as French had planned them. In spring one path blooms with borders of pink and white tree peonies and in summer with huge white hydrangea trees.

The other path is bordered by a confetti of color all summer long—irises, tulips, crimson phlox, hot pink hollyhocks, foxgloves, globe thistles, delphiniums, madonna lilies, asters.

French strolled and conferred along these paths, often puttering in the garden for an hour after breakfast and before supper. Because many of his commissions were outdoor sculptures for parks and cemeteries, he often worked in the garden testing the pieces in shadow and light. In July 1911, he wrote:

> The garden is as beautiful as a fairyland here now. The hemlocks are decorating themselves with their light green tassels and the laurel is beginning to blossom and the peonies are a glory in the garden. I go about in an ecstasy of delight over the loveliness of things.

Regularly of a Friday afternoon, guests came to take tea. Wandering through the garden, they filled the green-carpeted "room" with color: gentlemen in boaters and linen suits, ladies in white dotted swiss, their leghorn hats afloat with pastel ribbons. Isadora Duncan visited. The neighboring Choates came over from Naumkeag, as did Edith Wharton from The Mount. She would wander about the grounds with French, "exchanging ideas" and, according to Mrs. French, was

*

PRECEDING PAGE: *The garden path looking toward the studio, one of Daniel Chester French's favorite views of his garden.*

"courteous enough to ask his advice but artistic enough to need little from anyone."

By the pale light of Chinese lanterns, the Frenches entertained each summer with an annual costume ball, always a high point of the Berkshire summer social season.

For solitude, there were long walks through the forest, planned by French, who cut two woodland paths to "wild and natural vistas," considered to be "uplifting." Along the paths, French planted bloodroots, trilliums, wild sunflowers, periwinkles, and Canterbury bells.

The paths meander through thick woods and pass through sunlit glades filled with brilliant green ostrich ferns growing waist-high. Ultimately, each path emerges at an overlook with a view of the Berkshire hills. Wave upon wave of shimmering green recedes into blue haze.

Farmlands were considered suitable as a foreground on country estates, so French shaved off a hill behind the studio to make a rolling meadow. There he stationed three Jersey cows and dug a deep trench, called a ha-ha, to keep the cows from wandering too close to the house. The ha-ha was thought to be preferable to a fence, which would interrupt the flow of the vista from meadow to Monument Mountain.

Daniel Chester French was 38 when he married his witty, bon vivant first cousin, Mary. Eyebrows were raised at this consanguine union. But French was already a celebrated sculptor and a member of the Social Register. Mary's family was socially and politically prominent. These connections, plus their social gregariousness, ensured them a central place in Berkshire society.

For six months each year, the couple and their only child, Margaret, lived at their beloved Chesterwood. In 1969 Margaret donated 120 acres, the studio, house, and garden to the National Trust for Historic Preservation. Little has changed from the time when the Frenches were in residence.

CHESTERWOOD, PO Box 827, Stockbridge, MA 01262. (413) 298-3579. Owned by the National Trust for Historic Preservation.

OPEN
Grounds, studio, and house, May through October, daily, 10 A.M. to 5 P.M. Admission fee.

FACILITIES
· Picnicking permitted.
· Gift shop.

- Limited access for people with physical disabilities. Persons requiring special assistance should telephone for specific information.

EVENTS
- Daily, exhibitions and introductory slide show in Barn Gallery.
- Tours, daily, but group tours by reservation only.
- Antique Auto Show, Sunday, Memorial Day weekend.
- Outdoor Sculpture Show, July through October.
- Christmas at Chesterwood, a weekend in early November.

DIRECTIONS
Henry Hudson Parkway north to Saw Mill River Parkway to Taconic State Parkway. Take the Taconic to the end, then pick up the New York State Thruway, exiting at B/3 Berkshire Extension (Route 22). Route 22 branches almost immediately to Route 102. Take Route 102 east about 7 miles to Route 183. Turn right (south) and travel 1 mile to Chesterwood sign. Turn right and follow signs for ½ mile to entrance.

ᔗ

THE MOUNT

LENOX, MASSACHUSETTS

ᔗ With impeccable social connections in both New York and the Berkshires, novelist Edith Wharton wrote bitingly of the heart—and often the heartlessness—of upper-class Victorian society.

In this society, country houses with elaborate gardens were *de rigeur*. Edith Wharton and her husband, Teddy, were completing their summer retreat in the Berkshires when *Century Magazine* asked Mrs. Wharton to write a travel series on Italian villas and their gardens. Maxwell Parrish would do the color illustrations.

Italianate gardens were already in vogue on the estates of Newport and Long Island. Mrs. Wharton's articles, published as a book in 1904, became a classic in the genre of garden literature of the day.

As in Italian villas, the gardens designed by Mrs. Wharton for The Mount were an extension of the house, incorporating such Italianate elements as topiary promenades, pools, fountains, and a formal walled garden that looked out upon a wild, natural landscape. After all, the Berkshires and Tuscany shared much in common: lake-studded, hilly country with sweeping vistas that disappeared into blue horizons.

At The Mount, Edith's writing room opened, as it does now, onto a masonry terrace and commanded a view of two broad grass terraces descending to an allée of linden trees. The allée, called the Lime Walk because lindens smell like limes, connected two gardens. At one end was the Red Garden, a huge, open, sun-drenched square—100 feet by 110 feet—filled with fuchsia and red and pink flowers.

At the other end of the Lime Walk was Mrs. Wharton's *giardino segreto* (secret garden).

The gardens and the Lime Walk are slowly being restored according to a master plan prepared by Harvard's Graduate School of Design.

In the Red Garden, as in Mrs. Wharton's day, four L-shaped parterres will border a rectangular pond. Flower beds 12 feet wide will run around the perimeter of the garden. Mrs. Wharton called the Red Garden her "Oriental carpet floating in the sun." Of it she wrote her friend Sara Norton in July 1904:

> I have so been wishing you might see my garden lately. It is really what I thought it never could be a "mass of bloom." Ten varieties of phlox, some very gorgeous, are flowering together and then the snapdragons, lilacs and crimson stocks, penstemons, annual pinks in every shade of rose, salmon, cherry and crimson. . . . With the background of hollyhocks of every shade, from pale rose to dark red, it looks for a fleeting moment, like a garden in some civilized climate.

After the restoration, the Lime Walk will lead from the Red Garden to three small terraces—all-green anterooms that descend to the Italian Garden. Each will be planted with grass and walled with hedges of hemlock and arborvitae—a carefully calibrated contrast to the scale of the Italian Garden, an 80-foot square enclosed by 10-foot walls of stone and hedge.

White roses and white petunias will be planted in the four quadrants around a circular fountain. The stone wall on the lakeside is pierced by six arched openings that frame the daisied meadow and Laurel Lake beyond. A stone pergola in the middle of the wall provides the garden's only exit to the meadow. Entwined with grapevines, the pergola is a perfect place for taking tea.

Beatrix Jones Farrand, Edith Wharton's niece, was already enjoying minor success as a landscape architect when she designed the approach to The Mount, a distance of half a mile. Here, too, Farrand followed the style of an Italian country villa. All the working aspects—stable, barn, sheds, vineyards—were left exposed for all to see, a style in contradiction to the English great park tradition then in vogue where exposure of the mundane functions of an estate was considered gauche. This penchant for concealment behind fancy facades once led Mark

Twain to quip that American houses all had Queen Victoria fronts and Aunt Mary behinds.

The approach to The Mount led past stable, barns, and kitchen gardens on both sides of the road through an allée of sugar maples (Farrand preferred to use indigenous plants), then crisscrossed a woodsy brook before entering the graveled forecourt of The Mount.

The restoration of The Mount and gardens began in the 1970s when a developer who was converting the house and stable to rental units ran out of money. Lila Berle, a longtime neighbor who as a child had ridden her horse over to The Mount, galvanized community support and engineered a $300,000 mortgage loan for the 49 acres and house from the Endangered Properties Program of the National Trust for Historic Preservation.

By the summer of 1989 all masonry work is scheduled to be finished, and background plantings will be in place. By 1990, at a projected cost of $3 million (including $2.5 million for the house, $35,000 for the Red Garden, and $100,000 for the walled Italian Garden), the restoration will be complete.

THE EDITH WHARTON RESTORATION AT THE MOUNT, PO Box 974, Lenox, MA 01240. (413) 637-1899.

OPEN
Daily except Monday, June through Labor Day, 10 A.M. to 5 P.M.; last tour, 4 P.M. From Labor Day through October, Friday, Saturday, and Sunday, 10 A.M. to 5 P.M.; Columbus Day, 10 A.M. to 5 P.M. Admission fee.

FACILITIES
· Picnicking permitted.
· Gift shop.
· House accessible to people with physical disabilities; gardens have very limited access.

EVENTS
· October Dog Show, usually Columbus Day weekend. Admission fee.
· Luncheon benefit and auction of services (such as use of vacation houses, cooking a gourmet meal), last Sunday in June. Admission fee.
· Edith Wharton Plays, early July through Labor Day; Tuesday through Friday, 1 P.M.; Saturday, 1 P.M. and 4 P.M.; Sunday, 10 A.M. and 1 P.M. Admission fee.

- Periodic seminars on Edith Wharton and subjects relating to her life. Admission fee.
- Berkshire Cottage Tours, including Naumkeag and Chesterwood, beginning mid-July and ending Labor Day. Thursday, Friday, and Saturday at 9:30 A.M. and 2 P.M.; Sunday, 9:30 A.M. Some weekends in September and October. Admission fee.

DIRECTIONS
Henry Hudson Parkway north to Saw Mill River Parkway to Taconic State Parkway. Take the Taconic to the end to Exit 2 (Lee/Lenox). Take Route 20 north about 4 miles. Pass Laurel Lake on left and watch for blue and white sign to The Mount. Turn left onto Plunkett Street and go about ¾ of a mile to white gates on left.

NAUMKEAG

STOCKBRIDGE,

MASSACHUSETTS

The gardens at Naumkeag reflect two eras and the two women who shaped them: Caroline Choate and her daughter, Mabel. Both hired distinguished landscape architects. In 1885 Nathaniel Barrett designed and laid out the grounds of Naumkeag, and in 1925 Fletcher Steele reshaped them.

Together, the four built a garden that blends elements of an English great park, the baroque formalities of the Gilded Age, and the archplayfulness of the 1920s.

To Caroline, the family was the centerpiece of Naumkeag. To Mabel, who never married, the garden became central to her life.

Caroline sought a garden that would provide her husband, Joseph, with a backdrop appropriate to his position as an influential lawyer, ambassador, and diplomat. Naumkeag was also to be his refuge.

Mabel, art connoisseur and patron, sought a more comfortable and sparkling garden, one better suited to the private, casual life of the 1920s.

Through the years both women traveled widely, borrowing garden traditions from the Continent, England, and the Orient. Despite these foreign infusions, Naumkeag remains indelibly American. There is a bounty of color, a generosity of scale, a "permitted" unruliness in plantings that is delightfully homespun.

The gardens and house are sited on a steep hill overlooking a valley and the distant Berkshires. "The view," Fletcher Steele once wrote, "controls all things at Naumkeag." Cows graze in the hay meadow far below, where once the athletic fields and the family vegetable and cutting gardens were laid out in geometric precision. An apple orchard climbs the hill toward the house. In autumn the valley is rimmed with the fiery colors produced so gloriously by New England hardwood forests.

Caroline and Joseph were both exuberant people, devoted to each other and their children. They were in midlife when they assembled the 48 acres on the western slope of Prospect Hill. Prosperous and sociable, they created gardens for entertainment, display, and, to a lesser extent, recreation. Joseph, a scholarly lawyer who knew no peer in cross-examination, made a fortune representing America's rising industrial aristocracy, litigating such landmark cases as the New York Indians' land claims against the federal government, the Chinese Exclusion Act, and the Bell Telephone patent.

The Choates commissioned Stanford White, then 32 years old, to design their house, a shingled, turreted Norman-style mansion of 26 rooms, modest by Stockbridge standards.

Believing that "a formal garden is a gem . . . a pendant to the main house . . . [but] never part of the general scene," Nathaniel Barrett designed a two-tier garden north of the house, divided by a formal topiary evergreen walk. Below the house he graded the steep hill into grassy terraces, "splendid for social fetes." They were also splendid for family picnics, for children to roll down, for a croquet field and a grass tennis court.

After summer tours through Germany, in the 1890s Caroline planted a linden allée.

What can be seen of Caroline and Nathaniel Barrett's gardens

❧

PRECEDING PAGE: *Caroline Choate's Evergreen Walk, laid out at a "discreet" distance from the mansion.*

today are the Evergreen Walk and the linden allée, both badly battered by the freak snowstorm of October 1987, and the Lower Garden.

The Evergreen Walk—two rows of majestic arborvitae—was planted and pruned to look like Italian cypress, Italian villa gardens being much in vogue in the 1880s and 1890s, and cypress being a tree that does not take kindly to New England winters. Over the years, the arborvitae have grown fat and oval. The path between them is now so narrow that only two people can walk abreast.

The Evergreen Walk leads past Caroline's Lower Garden. The hemlock hedge once was clipped to look like a crenellated castle wall after the Choates returned from England where Joseph was ambassador. Now it is a solid wall, encircling a small pond and cast-iron benches. Partially obscured by a tangle of vines and brush, the ruins of a pergola makes this a romantic private enclosure. The Evergreen Walk ends at a white-water brook that plunges downhill under a canopy of shoulder-high ferns.

The lindens are tattered and in need of replacement now, but they still make a noble arch over a broad mossy path, a joy to walk through barefoot. Glimpses of the valley below punctuate this cool corridor.

Naumkeag harbored its tragedies, too. Of five children, two died in their youth and one lived out his adult years in a sanitarium. Only Joseph, Jr., and Mabel lived to a normal old age. Mabel inherited Naumkeag when she was 54 years old. The year was 1929, but she had begun to make changes in the gardens while her mother was still alive and summering there.

The changes began after Mabel met Fletcher Steele in 1925 at the Lenox Garden Club where he was giving a lecture. She invited him home. He came—and stayed for the next 30 summers while the two of them literally reshaped the Naumkeag landscape. They recontoured the south lawn and a neighboring woods—topping some trees as much as 20 feet so that both contours would replicate the profile of Bear Mountain in the distance. (This sculptured profile of the woods has long been overgrown.)

Fletcher Steele converted the broad, steep-sloped lawns—which took two men two days a week to mow—into more "manageable" terraces with stone masonry retaining walls. Today, espaliered apple trees and wisteria vines sun against the walls, and the terraces are planted with Oriental tree peonies. Just north of the terraces is the Rose Garden. Set in grass, scallop-shaped beds of pink, yellow, and red floribundas interlace with curving paths of salmon-colored gravel.

In 1926, Mabel returned from California much impressed with "outdoor rooms." She wanted a West Coast-style patio for Naumkeag, and to pep up the somber green plantings around the house. So Fletcher designed a Venetian-style afternoon tea terrace south of the house. He enclosed two sides of this Afternoon Garden with Venetian gondola posts, painted gold, turquoise, and salmon, and then linked them with ropes of clematis and Virginia creeper. The terrace, according to Steele, needed a "giddy" carpet. So he sank an oval pool lined with black glass in the center of the terrace, then looped it with a French knot garden of boxwood, pink and green stones, and black coal lumps.

In her travels to the Orient, Mabel collected Chinese Lowestoft porcelain, now displayed in the house. Lions, Buddhas, and dogs carved from stone can be seen in the Chinese walled garden.

To reach her cutting gardens, Mabel had to make a steep descent to the valley below. Why not make this 15-minute walk a pleasure in itself? Taking measure from the steep-hilled water gardens of Tuscany, Steele designed a water staircase. A translucent ribbon of water runs down a narrow channel in the middle of a brick staircase, then disappears into recessed pools at four landings. Each landing is outlined with Art Deco curved pipe railings, painted white. The staircase descends through a hillside of paper white birches, clustered in delicate fan-shaped groves of two and three. The dappled sunlight filtering down through the birches and the gentle sluicing of the water make the Birch Walk one of the most delicious garden experiences at Naumkeag.

NAUMKEAG, PO Box 792, Stockbridge, MA 01262. (413) 298-3239. Property of the Trustees of Reservations.

OPEN
- Gardens, daily, Memorial Day weekend through Columbus Day, 10 A.M. to 5 P.M.
- House, Memorial Day weekend through Columbus Day, Saturday, Sunday, holidays, and last Tuesday in June through Labor Day, daily except Monday, 10 A.M. to 4:15 P.M. Guided house tours. Admission fee.

FACILITIES
- Picnicking permitted.
- House not accessible to people with physical disabilities; most paths on grounds are unpaved.

EVENTS
Christmas at Naumkeag during even-numbered years, second weekend in December, 10 A.M. to 4 P.M. Admission fee.

DIRECTIONS

Henry Hudson Parkway north to Saw Mill River Parkway to Taconic State Parkway. Take Taconic to the end, and pick up Massachusetts Turnpike east. Exit at West Stockbridge. Take Route 102 east 9 miles to Stockbridge. Go through village. Across from Red Lion Inn, turn right onto Pine Street. Proceed a few blocks and bear left at a fork, onto Prospect Hill Road. Naumkeag is ½ mile from the Red Lion Inn on the left side of Prospect Hill Road. Entrance is second gate.

RHODE ISLAND

❧

BLITHEWOLD
GARDENS AND
ARBORETUM

BRISTOL, RHODE ISLAND

❧ Blithewold means "happy woodlands" in Middle English. That it is and more. On a finger of land that sticks out into Narragansett Bay, this country estate is 33 acres of sweeping vistas, flower gardens, a bosquet, rock and water gardens, and a rose garden, all punctuated with full-grown specimen trees.

The woodlands run parallel to the great lawn, a pathway to the sea that stretches for half a mile from the 45-room stone mansion.

Augustus VanWickle, who made his money from Pennsylvania coal mines, bought Blithewold in 1894 to provide a mooring in Bristol Harbor for his new steam yacht. He named the yacht the *Marjorie* for his 10-year-old daughter. The next year he hired John DeWolfe, landscape architect for the Borough of Brooklyn, to redesign the grounds of his estate. When VanWickle was killed in a skeet shooting accident, DeWolfe continued to mold Blithewold's landscape under the direction of VanWickle's widow, Bessie.

For the next 80 years, Bessie and later Marjorie, by then Mrs. George Lyon, continued to embellish the grounds. Mrs. Lyon opened the gardens to the public every Fourth of July for the rest of her life. She was 93 when she died, and in her will, she decreed that funds were to be spent first on maintenance of the grounds. Only then could any excess be spent on the house.

Of the seven gardens at Blithewold, the high points are the enclosed garden and the bosquet.

The enclosed garden is a green cocoon shut off from everything else, peaceful and complete. You enter through a small gap in the shrubbery to find that the frame is the focus of this garden, rather than the picture it encloses. False cypresses, hemlocks, and huge rhododendrons—the "frame"—form thick walls around a square of grass—the "picture." Specimen trees—a tiny-leaved weeping pagoda tree, an umbrella pine, a Pacific yew, and a giant sequoia 85 feet tall—are planted just far enough inside the dark green walls to display their individual shapes and colors.

The bosquet, on the other hand, is a magic forest, open and airy. Titania and Oberon might have lived in the seductive shade of this ethereal grove of thinned-out trees and rhododendrons. Beneath the trees, a rich carpet of myrtle, Solomon's-seal, ferns, and mayapples shimmers in spring with 18,000 daffodils.

Outside the bosquet, unrelated to anything else in the landscape, is a stand of yellow bamboo, originally grown to provide stakes for the garden. It grew and grew, until it cannibalized the cold frames nearby. Today it is so thick you can barely put an arm between the canes. In the blazing sun, only a glimpse of its dark and mysterious center is visible.

Nearby is the cutting garden, plain in layout but not in color—delicious lemony pink California poppies, scarlet bee balm, deep pink phlox, lavender germander, pale yellow marigolds—bed after bed with a hodgepodge of color and species. In the middle, pinkish plume grass and gray-leaved santolina edge a water lily pool.

The north garden, designed to be viewed from the mansion, was once a formal nineteenth-century garden, with gravel paths and parterres edged with box. Now greatly shrunk, the garden is still pretty. Perennials, mostly blue and yellow, are set out around a small pool and fountain. There are hibiscus, lilies, balloon flowers, coreopsis, flax, Russian sage, globe thistle, monkshood, and veronica.

Something is always in flower from early spring to November in the rock garden, which volunteers meticulously label and maintain. Large stands of Japanese anemones and astilbes grow among lobelias, crested gentians, carpets of sedums, and glossy European ginger.

In the water garden, a giant weeping willow hangs over two small pools connected by a curved stone bridge. Bristol Harbor glitters in the distance. From the water garden, a grassy path cuts a swath to the beach—wading permitted—through light woods high with wildflowers.

BLITHEWOLD GARDENS AND ARBORETUM, 101 Ferry Road (Route 114), Bristol, RI 02809. (401) 253-2707. Owned by the Heritage Foundation of Rhode Island.

OPEN
- Grounds, daily, 10 A.M. to 4 P.M. Admission fee.
- Mansion, mid-April through October, 10 A.M. to 4 P.M.; all furnishings are original. Admission fee.

FACILITIES
- Picnicking permitted.
- Gift shop.
- Mansion not accessible to wheelchairs; grounds have limited accessibility, no paved paths.

EVENTS
- Valentine's Day (nearest Saturday) chamber music concert. Admission fee.
- Spring plant sale, Saturday before Mother's Day.
- Concerts by the Bay, June to Labor Day, 2 outdoor and 5 indoor concerts, varied music. Admission fee.
- Christmas at Blithewold, 2 weeks in December, special decorations and 20-foot tree, Christmas shop. Admission fee.
- Courses on horticultural and historical subjects, lectures, and workshops given periodically, year-round. Admission fee.

DIRECTIONS
Triborough Bridge to Bruckner Expressway (I-278) to New England Thruway (Route 95) to Exit 3 (in Rhode Island). Take Route 138 east across Jamestown Bridge and across Newport Bridge. From Newport, take Route 114 north across Mt. Hope Bridge; bear left at fork onto Ferry Road (Route 114). Blithewold is ¼ mile ahead on the left.

GREEN
ANIMALS

~~ You know Green Animals is going to be wonderful the minute you turn into the parking lot. Everything looks so pretty and fresh. Beds of flaming orange Mexican sunflowers run along the white board fence. Beyond a giant beech and a gleaming white-clapboard house, Narragansett Bay is visible in the distance.

Next to the house are 2½ acres of gardens and topiaries of animals and ornamental shapes—a bear, a rooster, a peacock, a swan, and a unicorn, pillars and carved arches—80 sculptures in all. Some animals stand at attention. Others cavort and gambol amid the flower beds like pets at play. They are amusing and amazing.

Tall topiary columns—some plain, some spiraled like giant screws—line one side of a formal parterre garden. Giraffe, camel, elephant, and lion topiaries survey the garden in lordly silence.

Boxwood outlines beds of many shapes, each filled with a different flower—rose-colored zinnias, violet impatiens, pink begonias, and yellow snapdragons. The pale pink plumes of fountain grass wave in a border around the perimeter of the parterre garden.

Green Animals is famous for its topiary, but it is the flower beds that produce the exuberance. Thirty-five beds, square and oblong-shaped, line up one right after the other, separated by narrow paths. Color is the key, combinations of color. In one bed, blackish purple salvia mixes with dark 'Purple Ruffle' basil and white snapdragons touched with fuchsia. In another, lavender phlox and white phlox are bordered by crimson achillea. In a third, downy beige wands of the grass *Pennisetum villosum* float like moths above pink, maroon, and white cosmos.

Peach trees dot a number of the beds, the remainders of orchards that once covered the property. One bed holds richly fruiting fig trees. (They lean as though tipsy, not from the weight of the fruit but from being pushed to the ground each winter and then buried under mounds of soil for protection.)

Annuals predominate, grown from seed in the garden's green-house. Three perennial beds, only a few years old, are filling in nicely with a number of unusual cultivars, including grasses.

Something is going on wherever you look. Water lilies—from amethyst and green to deep rose and purple—goldfish, carp, papyrus, and lotus garnish a small pool. Nearby are two arbors, one hung with ornamental gourds and the other with four varieties of grapes, each a different color. A large bed exhibits All-America Selections Winners, new varieties of award-winning annual flowers. A stand of giant reed grass, 12 feet high, looks like Brobdingnagian cornstalks. The grass is cut each fall and made into fences to protect the topiaries from winter winds.

Superintendent Ernie Wasson and his assistant, Tricia Dougherty, start trimming the topiary in May. Five summer helpers join in the trimming, which continues till mid-September. Only Ernie trims the yew rooster and teddy bear. Yew gets only two cuts a year, and he wants to control the shape. Boxwood gets two cuts each season. But privet, the third shrub commonly used for topiary, is much more demanding—every two weeks when young, every three to four weeks when mature.

The topiary was started by a Portuguese gardener hired by Thomas Brayton, a textile mill owner who summered here from the 1870s to

❧

PRECEDING PAGE: *A topiary teddy bear made of yew.*

219

1917. After Brayton's death, his daughter, Alice, moved here from Fall River and made her debut in nearby Newport society. She was then 61 years old. Green Animals, a name she chose, became her entrée into that society.

At Christmas parties, lawn fetes, and clambakes, families and children frolicked among the whimsical topiaries. An invitation to Green Animals was highly prized; the topiary was a lure that helped Alice Brayton maintain her social position for over 30 years.

A bad winter in 1928 killed all the topiary. The Portuguese gardener, José Carreiro, began again, and a number of the topiary animals date from that time. The old style was to grow them from a single plant, but the new style is to start with more plants. A dog, for example, would begin with four plants for the legs. As new stems emerge, they are pushed and pulled, trained, interwoven, and repositioned into shape. They are pruned, and pruned again, as many as nine times a season. No wires or frames are used, and weather is always a danger. The giraffe was five feet taller before the last hurricane.

In summer, 10 small, green wooden rockers made in animal shapes cluster under a pine tree on the lawn. Children can ride a hippo, an elephant, or a giraffe. As in Alice Brayton's day, families picnic at nearby tables. At the end of the lane that leads to Green Animals visitors alight from the two-car train that comes from Newport once a day during the spring and summer.

GREEN ANIMALS, Cory's Lane (off Route 114), Portsmouth, RI 02871. (401) 683-1267. Owned by the Preservation Society of Newport County, 118 Mill Street, Newport, RI 02840.

OPEN
May through September, daily, 10 A.M. to 5 P.M.; October, weekends and holidays, 10 A.M. to 5 P.M. Groups of 20 or more may receive a group discount if reservations are made in advance; call (401) 847-6543. Admission fee.

FACILITIES
· Picnicking permitted.
· Doll museum in house; included in admission fee.
· Gift and plant shop.
· Garden is accessible to people with physical disabilities; gravel and dirt paths. House has limited accessibility.

DIRECTIONS

Triborough Bridge to Bruckner Expressway (I-278) to New England Thruway (Route 95) to Exit 3 (in Rhode Island). Take Route 138 east across Jamestown Bridge and across Newport Bridge. From Newport, take Route 114 north about 10 miles to Cory's Lane on the left. (There is a stoplight at Cory's Lane.) Turn left, and Green Animals is at the end of the lane on the left.

The Old Colony & Newport Railway leaves Newport each afternoon for its regular 9½-mile once-a-day trip along Narragansett Bay. The route ends at Cory's Lane at Green Animals. There the train rests for an hour before returning to Newport. Two vintage passenger cars—from the late 1800s and the turn of the century—views of unspoiled beaches, and the leisurely speed create a feeling of long ago. The train operates Sundays in May and June and on Memorial Day; daily, July through Labor Day. Call (401) 294-4153/849-5530 for details.

꒜

HAMMERSMITH
FARM

NEWPORT, RHODE ISLAND

꒜ The weathered gray-shingled house, a mass of curves, towers, and turrets, is over a hundred years old, large, and homey. Jacqueline Bouvier spent childhood summers here. On the lawn overlooking Narragansett Bay, she danced with John F. Kennedy at their wedding reception.

This former summer home of Kennedy's in-laws is now owned and run as a tourist attraction by Camelot Gardens. The name says it all—the house and its Kennedy associations are the magnet for tourists. Within this commercial framework, Camelot Gardens has been a decent garden steward, renovating and maintaining flower borders.

But the main horticultural reason to visit Hammersmith Farm is the vestigial remains of gardens created by Frederick Law Olmsted. After 90 years they still have their own pull.

The strongest elements of the original Olmsted design remain: some stone structures and a long line of allées—two of lindens and one of Japanese cedars.

The allées begin near the house and progress in a straight line to a stone boundary wall. Filtered light sifts through the first allée of bluish green Japanese cedars. The gravel path that unrolls between the tall, delicate-needled trees continues through a stone arch. Beyond the arch, the furrowed gray trunks and round clipped heads of silver lindens form two shorter allées, separated by a broad expanse of grass.

The stretch of grass is empty except for a small semicircle of dusty miller, begonia, and ageratum, out of scale and forlorn. Something is obviously missing. It is the lily pond in the shape of a four-leaf clover, 40 feet across, that was filled in during World War II. The pond bridged the space, linking the allées of silver lindens.

In the woods opposite, another Olmsted stone arch still stands, hidden under a mantle of vines and shrubbery.

Near the house, trim terrace gardens reflect the colors—yellow, pink, heliotrope, white, blue, and green—of the master bedroom that overlooks them. Annuals and some perennials are pleasantly arranged over two levels. On the lower level, a pergola covered with Concord grapevines provides a cool place to sit and a view of the bay.

Enormous cutting gardens located in a back corner of the property provide flowers for the house. There should be enough left over to decorate half of Newport. Over 100 varieties, mostly annuals, are jammed row upon row in a brilliant field of color.

HAMMERSMITH FARM, Ocean Drive, Newport, RI 02840. (401) 846-7346.

OPEN

Daily, April through October; weekends, March and November; Memorial Day weekend through Labor Day, 10 A.M. to 7 P.M.; spring and fall, 10 A.M. to 5 P.M. Admission fee includes entrance to grounds and guided tour of the mansion.

FACILITIES
· Gift shop.
· Gardens accessible to people with physical disabilities; unpaved paths. Limited accessibility to first floor of house.

EVENTS
Newport Music Festival, July, classical music. Admission fee.

DIRECTIONS
Triborough Bridge to Bruckner Expressway (I-278) to New England Thruway (Route 95) north to Exit 3 (in Rhode Island). Take Route 138 east across Jamestown Bridge and across Newport Bridge. Follow signs for Ocean Drive and Fort Adams State Park, which is next to Hammersmith Farm.

INDEX

PHOTO CREDITS

The authors gratefully acknowledge permission to use the following photographs: page 5, John Calabrese; page 11, Metropolitan Museum of Art; pages 15, 36, 41, 58, 64, 73, Gita Dunhill; page 20, Allen Rokach; page 44, Richard Cheek; page 68, Bonnie Fiero; page 101, Anne Ross; page 109, Cyrus Hyde; page 132, Joanna Reed; page 139, Longwood Gardens, Inc.; page 149, David Haas, Morris Arboretum of the University of Pennsylvania; page 163, Alice Bissell; page 181, Lynn Sadlon; page 199, Chesterwood Museum, Stockbridge, Massachusetts, a property of the National Trust for Historic Preservation; page 207, Clemens Kalischer; page 218, the Preservation Society of Newport County.